JANU
PER

DEUTERONOMY

A CHALLENGE

TO A NEW GENERATION

LifeWay Press®
Nashville, TN

ISBN: 978-1-4300-3182-6
Item: 005643513

Subject Area: Bible Studies
Dewey Decimal Classification Number: 222.15
Subject Heading: DEUTERONOMY—STUDY \ FAITH \ OBEDIENCE
Printed in the United States of America

Adult Ministry Publishing
LifeWay Church Resources
One LifeWay Plaza
Nashville, TN 37234-0175

We believe the Bible has God for its author; salvation for its end; and truth, without any mixture of error, for its matter and that all Scripture is totally true and trustworthy. To review LifeWay's doctrinal guidelines, please visit *www.lifeway.com/doctrinalguideline*.

Lesson Photos: Biblical Illustrator Photos

CONTENTS

COVER IMAGE: ISTOCK PHOTO

INTRODUCTION

A CHALLENGE TO A NEW GENERATION

In 1991, I moved my family from a wonderful church in Gardendale, Alabama, to serve as the pastor of Green Acres Baptist Church in Tyler, Texas. I'm still serving the Lord with these wonderful folks. But my wife and I discovered what a challenge it is to move to a new state and start over again. We had to find a house and have utilities put in our names. We had to get Texas tags and Texas driver's licenses. We had to find new doctors and dentists—and most importantly, for my wife, a new hairstylist!

Starting over is always a challenge. You might have moved to a new city and faced the challenges we faced. Or you might have gone through the heartache of divorce or the grief of the death of a spouse. Suddenly, you found yourself struggling to start over. There are many occasions in our lives when we are called on to start over.

When you open the Book of Deuteronomy, you meet an entire nation that is starting over again with the challenge of entering the promised land. After the action and narrative of Exodus and Numbers, we find the massive mob of Hebrews camped at the northern edge of the Sinai Wilderness. This new generation is once again poised to enter the land in which their parents had never set foot, though they had scouted it out 40 years earlier. The older, rebellious generation had made the mistake of not trusting God's power and promise at Kadesh-barnea. As they wandered around in the wilderness, their dreams died along with their bodies, leaving their bones to bleach beneath the desert sun.

God's leader, Moses, is now 120 years old, yet he still has the strength and vigor of a young man (Deut. 34:7). Before he places the mantle of leadership on his replacement, Joshua, he is inspired by the Holy Spirit to repeat many of the laws and commands of God to this new generation. Deuteronomy is his final message to this new generation as they prepare to claim God's promises. According to one Hebrew division of the book, Deuteronomy contains eight "orations" or "sermons" that Moses delivered to the people. Early in my ministry I preached at an old fashioned, outdoor camp meeting that went on for eight nights. Since the Israelites are camped out in the Jordan Valley, you might think of Deuteronomy as an eight-night camp meeting led by Moses.

Above: This workman's village in Medinet Habu, Egypt may have been a complex similar to what the Israelites lived in as slaves to pharaoh.

ILLUSTRATOR PHOTO/ BOB SCHATZ (16/27/15)

ALL OF THE BIBLE IS GOD-BREATHED

Of course, we believe in the miracle of the inspiration of the Bible. But there is also the miracle of the compilation of the Bible. Forty individuals speaking different languages wrote the Bible over a period of 1,600 years, yet there is a miraculous unity in the way the 66 books are compiled.

The five writings of Moses comprise the Pentateuch, which is actually the entire Bible in miniature. Genesis reports the fall of humanity because of sin. In Exodus we discover the redemption that comes from the blood of the lamb. In Leviticus we learn of the communion we can have with a Holy God through atonement. In Numbers we see how God guides us and provides for us through the times of personal wilderness. In Deuteronomy we are reminded of God's faithfulness even when we are disobedient to His commands. Deuteronomy is more than the final book of the Pentateuch; it reveals the beautiful completion of God's plan of redemption.

Just as the Old Testament begins with five historical books—Genesis to Deuteronomy—the New Testament begins the same way. There are striking similarities between the fifth book of the Old Testament, Deuteronomy, and the fifth book of the New Testament, the Acts of the Apostles. Both books describe a period of transition from the old to the new.

The structure of Deuteronomy is simple. Like many preachers, Moses had three points. Chapters 1–4 are a REFLECTION on God's love and care for Israel in the wilderness. The largest section of the book, chapters 5–26, contain a REVIEW of the laws of God. Chapters 27–34 contain a REVELATION of the future for Israel.

The Hebrew name for this fifth book is *Haddebharim,* which means "words." This comes from the beginning verse, "The words Moses spoke" (1:1). The Jewish rabbis often referred to this book as Mishneh Hattorah, which means "the repetition of the law." In the third century, when the Septuagint translators rendered the Old Testament into Greek, they picked up on this theme and named it Deuteronomion Touto or "Second Law." This Greek phrase led to the English translation "Deuteronomy."

But the fifth book of the Bible is much more than a repetition of the Law. It is the last word from a mighty man who spoke to God face-to-face and was called God's friend (Ex. 33:11). The book closes with Moses going up to Mount Nebo, which overlooked the land of Canaan. Because he had disobeyed God in striking the rock with a rod rather than speaking to it, Moses was not permitted to enter the land.

Some have called Deuteronomy Moses' extended epitaph. It contains the final testimony of the leader who was a mediator between God and the people. His constant intercession for these sinful people provides a clear foreshadowing of the Mediator of the New Covenant, the Lord Jesus Christ, who ever lives to make intercession for us (Heb. 7:25).

As we embark on our study of Deuteronomy, you'll soon discover the dual themes of the holiness and love of God. There is no contradiction between

God's absolute holiness and His infinite love. As believers, we are free from the Old Testament Law, but we can never escape the fact that God is holy and He requires holiness from His people.

There is no contradiction between God's absolute holiness and His infinite love.

Of course, as followers of Christ, we rejoice that only through His death on the cross can we be set free from the curse of sin. And it is only through His holy life lived in us that we can be holy. We can never "act holy" enough to please God. It is only through "Christ in you, the hope of glory" (Col. 1:27) that we can demonstrate true holiness.

I agree with Henrietta Mears who wrote about Deuteronomy: "Nothing in literature matches the majesty of its eloquence. No book in all the Word of God pictures better the life that is lived according to God's will and the blessings showered upon the soul who comes into

Left: The Torah Scroll found in Jerusalem.

ILLUSTRATOR PHOTO/ BOB SCHATZ/ ROYAL ONTARIO MUSEUM, TORONTO (29/15/6)

Below: The spring of Moses is the traditional Arabic site where Moses struck the rock. The spring is near Petra, Jordan.

ILLUSTRATOR PHOTO/ BOB SCHATZ (8/20/2)

the richness and fullness of spiritual living along the rugged pathway of simple obedience .... If you want a taste of heaven on earth, become familiar with Deuteronomy."[1]

OUR STUDY PLAN

Since Deuteronomy is such a comprehensive book, a verse-by-verse study will be impossible. So, we will be focusing instead on the major passages and themes. It is my prayer that you won't simply study Deuteronomy as a historical book. I pray that you will experience the truth found in these pages of God's Word.

Whenever you study any passage of the Bible, you are wise to consider three questions.

First, what did the passage mean to the original audience? You can call that INVESTIGATION.

Second, what are the general spiritual principles that can be drawn from the passage? That study is called INTERPRETATION.

And third, what is God saying to me? That step is called APPLICATION.

It's unfortunate that some Bible studies primarily focus on the first two questions. In this study, I hope that you will apply these truths to your life.

The same God who delivered the Hebrews from the bondage of slavery in Egypt is the God who has delivered us from the bondage of sin.

The Israelites' story is our story. The same God who delivered the Hebrews from the bondage of slavery in Egypt is the God who has delivered us from the bondage of sin. The blood of the Passover Lamb deflected God's fatal judgment, just as Christ, our Passover Lamb (1 Cor. 5:7), has absorbed God's justice in our place (Gal. 3:13). The Hebrew people were "baptized into Moses in the Dead Sea," and we have been baptized into Christ (1 Cor. 10:2). As God led them toward the promised land, they faced a variety of problems, obstacles, and enemies. Doesn't that sound like the Christian life we live? But contrary to some of the old hymns, Canaan isn't heaven, and we don't have to die physically to enter into God's promise. Canaan, a land flowing with milk and honey, is a picture of a life of spiritual warfare that is marked with victory that we achieve through our Joshua, Jesus. Everything happening in the Exodus experience is happening in our lives.

When you read your Bible using this key, it suddenly comes alive. An ancient book like Deuteronomy becomes more up-to-date than tomorrow's newspaper!

1. Henrietta C. Mears, *What the Bible is all About,* (Regal Books, 1953), pp. 74-75.

CHAPTER 1

GOD'S CHARACTER REVEALED

DEUTERONOMY 1:1–4:43

The first section of Deuteronomy reveals both the power and patience of God. The Israelites didn't have a copy of the Bible to read to learn about the character of God. They had something better than a book. They had the opportunity to witness God's loving provision for them and learn firsthand about His character.

As we begin our study, I encourage you to put yourself in the sandals of the Israelites. According to Numbers 1:46, the Hebrews numbered into the hundreds of thousands. There were more than 600,000 men, not counting their family members. Some scholars have estimated that the size of the wandering nation could have numbered as many as two million people. Marching 50 abreast, they would have formed a line 30 miles long!

Imagine yourself there with them, camped in the desert. Picture thousands of rows of pitched tents with the tabernacle of God placed in the center. Close your eyes and smell the smoke from ten thousand Hebrew campfires. Hear the discontented grunts from the herds of livestock traveling with them all day. Listen to the laughter of thousands of children playing between the tents at sunset. Then lift your eyes to the challenges that you face across the Jordan River in an unknown land called Canaan. It is indeed a challenge for every generation of Christians to claim God's promises by faith.

IT'S TIME TO MOVE FORWARD (DEUT. 1:1–18)

Have you ever taken a trip where you experienced delays? Late one night, while flying into Costa Rica, the San Jose airport was socked in by fog, and we were unable to land. The nearest alternate airport was in Managua, Nicaragua. We landed there after midnight, and the airport was closed and dark. Finally a couple of airport workers arrived and maneuvered the air stairs to the jet and we disembarked. We were not able to unload our luggage. There was a cheap hotel two blocks from the airport, so imagine 150 weary flyers walking in the dark to the hotel and lining up to check in with the single desk clerk who spoke very little English. I finally got to bed around 3:00 A.M., and was up early the next morning. The flight crew had exceeded their flying time, so a new crew had to be flown in, so we ended up waiting at the Managua airport all day. We finally arrived in

Costa Rica about 24 hours after our scheduled arrival. I had been scheduled to speak at the dedication service of a church building our men had constructed, and I missed it. You probably have experienced the frustration of travel delays.

But I have a hard time complaining about a 24-hour delay when I think about the 40-year delay the children of Israel experienced in their journey toward the promised land. Moses pointed out in Deuteronomy 1:2 that it was an 11-day journey from Horeb to Kadesh-barnea. A trip that could have taken 11 days instead took 40 years.

We can only imagine the joy and relief when God finally said, "You have stayed at this mountain long enough. Resume your journey" (Deut. 1:6-7). Remember, God's delays are not God's denials. With God, timing is much more critical than time. When Mary and Martha sent word to Jesus that their brother, Lazarus, was sick, He intentionally delayed His journey to Bethany. He knew that God would receive more glory from the resuscitation of a dead man than from the healing of a sick man. In the same way, the story of the Israelites reminds us that God wants to receive the greatest possible glory in our lives, and sometimes that involves waiting on His perfect timing.

In what area of your life have you experienced the frustration of delay?

How do you know when God is telling you to move forward in faith?

» LEARNING ACTIVITY

THE BOOK OF DEUTERONOMY

- Written by Moses; his last messages to Israel
- Written after the 40 years of wandering in the wilderness; written before entry into the promised land
- Themes addressed include:
  - The nature and character of God as highlighted in His holiness, sovereignty, graciousness, and love
  - The covenant relationship between God and His people
  - The response of faith by God's people to God
  - Sin and its consequences
- After the Books of Psalms and Isaiah, Deuteronomy is the most quoted Book in the New Testament.
- Jesus quoted from Deuteronomy three times while tempted by Satan in the wilderness (see Matt. 4:4-10).

Above: Kadesh-barnea

MATSON PHOTO/ LIBRARY OF CONGRESS

LEARN FROM YOUR PAST FAILURES (DEUT. 1:19-28)

As Moses looked back in time, he highlighted the biggest failure of the entire Exodus trip. The first generation had arrived at Kadesh-barnea, but they didn't trust God enough to enter into the promised land. As the late singer-songwriter, Keith Green, put it, God said, "Take another lap around Mount Sinai."

I've always suspected that the children of Israel acted like many churches today. They elected a Holy Land Investigation Committee of 12 men. Upon returning, 10 of the 12 members of the committee gave a majority report. They confirmed that it was indeed a rich land flowing with milk and honey, but that giants lived there. These 10 men suffered from a grasshopper-complex and spread fear among the Israelites that if they tried to take the land, they would be squashed like insects.

But two of the men, Caleb and Joshua, gave a minority report that confirmed that giants lived there. But they believed that God was bigger than any giant, so they encouraged the people to charge into the land and trust God. The 10 cowards said, "They're too big for us to attack!"

Joshua and Caleb said, "They're too big for us to miss!"

By the way, not many Christians can recall any of the names of the 10 spies who gave a negative report. All of them are mentioned in Numbers 13. However, all of us know the names of the two faith-filled spies. We proudly name our sons Joshua and Caleb, but we forget the names of those who show a lack of faith.

That day the Israelites voted against God, because the camp was filled with the crying and wailing of a people who were too fearful to trust God. Moses retold this story so that a younger generation could learn from the failure of their parents.

Have you experienced failure in your life? Maybe you've gone through the heartache of a failed marriage or a failed job; you got fired or were asked to resign. You might have applied for a scholarship or a job, and gotten turned down. You might be suffering from failing health, or you might have experienced a financial failure. Maybe you feel you failed as a parent or you failed in a business venture.

The lesson we learn from Deuteronomy is that failure doesn't have to be final. If you learn from your failures and refuse to quit, then your failures can become the fertilizer for future success.

The lesson we learn from Deuteronomy is that failure doesn't have to be final.

Who are some of the great leaders in the Bible who recovered from failure?

What key lessons have you learned from personal failure?

OUR GOD WILL CARRY US (DEUT. 1:29-46)

In recalling this pivotal event, Moses provided a wonderful picture of the loving character of God. When the Israelites rebelled against God, Moses tried to encourage them by saying,

> Don't be terrified or afraid of them! The LORD your God who goes before you will fight for you, just as you saw Him do for you in Egypt. And you saw in the wilderness how the LORD your God carried you as a man carries his son all along the way you traveled until you reached this place. But in spite of this you did not trust the LORD your God (1:29-32).

Let's be honest. We've all heard the worn-out story of "footprints in the sand" too many times. I won't repeat it, but you may recall it ends with God saying, "That's when I carried you." Actually, that story isn't far-fetched because Moses claimed that God carried them as a man carries his son.

That analogy should resonate with every parent or grandparent. I didn't have a son, but when I carried my little daughters, I did everything within my power to keep them safe from harm. Now I have a grandson, and I carry him with the same sense of love and protection.

God is still carrying us today. Will you trust His strong arms? In the next-to-last chapter of Deuteronomy, Moses reminded this generation again that "underneath are the everlasting arms" (33:27).

To paraphrase this promise to you, remember that the God who carried you this far is not going to let you down now. For those of us who know Jesus as our Savior, God has been carrying us since the moment we placed our lives in His hands. There hasn't been a single nanosecond that we have been out of His care.

The God who carried you this far is not going to let you down now.

When was a time that God carried you through a tough situation?

How did that experience impact your faith in Him?

GAIN CONFIDENCE FROM SMALLER VICTORIES (DEUT. 2:1–3:29)

A strange thing happened on the way to Canaan. This new generation encountered enemies before they ever made it to the Jordan River. Two strong kings stood in the way of their journey to the Promised Land. King Sihon of the Amorites tried to stop them. He attacked the Israelites. But this was an army that had learned to trust God.

Moses reported, "So Sihon and his whole army came out against us for battle at Jahaz. The Lord our God handed him over to us, and we defeated him, his sons, and his whole army" (2:32-33). Moses was careful to point out that the Israelites didn't win the battle themselves, but that God fought for them and gave them the victory.

Then they came to the land of Bashan, and King Og also refused to allow them to pass through his land. Another battle. Another victory. Again, Moses reported, "So the Lord our God also handed over Og king of Bashan and his whole army to us" (3:32).

The army of Israel captured 60 cities in Bashan. Moses gave this land to the tribes of Reuben, Gad, and the half-tribe of Manasseh. They would live on the east side of the Jordan, but the men were commanded to accompany the other tribes to fight for Canaan.

These were fortified cities, but they were small towns compared to Jericho. God gave the Israelites smaller victories so they would have confidence to trust Him in the big battles.

Moses made sure that Joshua learned this important lesson. He told him,

> Your own eyes have seen everything the Lord your God has done to these two kings. The Lord will do the same to all the kingdoms you are about to enter. Don't be afraid of them, for the Lord your God fights for you (3:21-22).

Big victories only come after we have experienced a series of smaller victories. If you are faithful and trust God when you face the smaller challenges—your personal Amorites, and Bashans—then you know you can trust Him for the Jericho's that you face. Jesus said, "Whoever is faithful in very little is also faithful in much, and whoever is unrighteous in very little is also unrighteous in much" (Luke 16:10). Have courage. Don't be afraid, because the Lord your God fights for you.

What are some of the obstacles you're facing now in your progress toward claiming God's promise?

How can you step forward in faith and claim victory?

DON'T FORGET WHAT YOU HAVE SEEN! (DEUT. 4:1-14)

I'm not a big fan of eating in a cafeteria. There are just too many choices, and I usually get more than I can eat. You have to stand in a slow moving line, but when you get to the food it seems that the line speeds up. I end up getting more than I can eat. It's not a relaxing experience, I prefer to sit down in a restaurant and order from a menu.

Sadly, some Christians seem to treat God's commands like a cafeteria line. They think you can pick and choose what they want to obey. The earlier generation of Israelites had suffered because they hadn't obeyed God. Moses warned this new generation about making the same mistake. He said,

> You must not add anything to what I command you or take anything away from it, so that you may keep the commands of the LORD your God I am giving you. Your eyes have seen what the LORD did at Baal-peor, for the LORD your God destroyed every one of you who followed Baal of Peor (4:2-3).

Sadly, some Christians seem to treat God's commands like a cafeteria line.

In addition to the danger of "cafeteria-style Christianity," some believers suffer from spiritual amnesia. They forget what God has done. Moses also warned against this malady. He said,

> Be on your guard and diligently watch yourselves, so that you don't forget the things your eyes have seen and so that they don't slip from your mind as long as you live. Teach them to your children and your grandchildren (4:9).

Hindsight isn't always 20/20 because we sometimes forget the past. Like the Israelites, each of us has a spiritual heritage. There are events in the past that have had an impact on our faith. There are people who have touched our lives in positive ways. We should never let this slip from our minds as long as we live.

Hindsight isn't always 20/20 because we sometimes forget the past.

We all have a spiritual legacy to leave as well. God commanded the Israelites to teach their children and grandchildren about His mighty acts. To this day, the Jewish people have a rich oral tradition of passing on the stories of their heritage. At every Passover meal, the story of God's miraculous liberation of the Jews from Egypt is repeated.

As a follower of Jesus, you should have stories of God's goodness as well. Are you faithful to pass them on to your children and grandchildren? The Bible says, "Sons are indeed a heritage from the Lord, children, a reward. Like arrows in the hand of a warrior are the sons born in one's youth" (Ps. 127:3-4). An arrow can be pointed and it can go where the warrior could never go. Our role as Christian parents is to point our children and grandchildren to Christ, and then to launch them into life with a rich spiritual legacy. The best thing you can leave them isn't money or property. The best thing you can leave them is a legacy of faith.

Why do you think it is important to leave a spiritual legacy?

What kind of legacy do you plan to leave your children and grandchildren after the Lord calls you home?

» LEARNING ACTIVITY

GOD'S JEALOUSY

"For the Lord your God is a consuming fire, a jealous God" (Deut. 4:24). God is jealous when we give to someone or something else what belongs to Him alone—especially our worship and service. Read the following verses and note how they describe God's jealousy:

Exodus 20:4-5

Psalm 135:4

Isaiah 42:8

James 4:4-5

WORSHIP THE ONE TRUE GOD! (DEUT. 4:15-40)

Can you recall a time in your life when you first became aware of the awesome power of God? I grew up in L.A. (Lower Alabama), and I never saw mountains until I took my first trip to Colorado as a college student. I'll never forget the impression I felt when I first gazed at a snow-capped mountain. I was reminded of the awesome majesty of our Creator who designed and made such a beautiful feature. That was truly a mountaintop experience.

The Israelites had experienced a mountaintop experience that no other nation could claim. They had the voice of God speaking from the fire on top of Mount Sinai. No doubt, some of this younger generation could remember that time. Moses reminded them that there is only one God. He said,

> You were shown these things so that you would know that the Lord is God; there is no other besides Him. ... Today, recognize and keep in mind that the Lord is God in heaven above and on earth below; there is no other (4:35,39).

There are many gods that people worship, but there is only one living God. Anything else is a dead idol. *American Idol* isn't just a popular show about undiscovered singers. America is full of idols. An idol is anyone or anything that occupies the place of God in your life.

Are you worshiping anything or anyone more than God? Give yourself the "four T test."

- *What do you think about the most?*
- *What do you talk about the most?*
- *What do you give your treasure to without regard of the cost?*
- *What do you devote your time to?*

If anything or anyone wins the "four T Test" other than God, then you may be a victim of idolatry.

What do your answers to the "four T test" reveal about your priorities?

A CLOSER LOOK

JESUS IS THE CITY OF OUR REFUGE
(Deut. 4:41-43)

"Then Moses set apart three cities across the Jordan to the east. Someone could flee there who committed manslaughter, killing his neighbor accidentally without previously hating him. He could flee to one of these cities and stay alive" (4:41-42).

God made an interesting provision for the Israelites who had accidentally killed another person. Certain cities were designated as "cities of refuge." These cities were established to provide protection against an "avenger of blood" (Josh. 20:3). A guilty (or non-guilty) person could flee the vengeance of relatives by fleeing to one of these cities where he would be protected until there could be a trial.

Those who found themselves inside the city walls were assured safety and freedom from those who sought their demise, while those found outside the city walls had nothing more than the uncertainty of their survival.

This is a wonderful foreshadowing of the refuge we find in Christ. We are all guilty of sin—both intentional and unintentional. We have no excuse. Jesus is a city of refuge who seeks the weary, wherever we are. In the clutches of sin, in the darkness—void of light, He is there; a city brightly lit.

We see this picture of Christ in Hebrews 6:18-19, "we who have fled for refuge might have strong encouragement to seize the hope set before us. We have this hope as an anchor for our lives, safe and secure." Our only hope is to flee to Christ. But rather than having to seek Him, our City of Refuge is seeking us.

CHAPTER 2

GOD'S CHARACTER REFLECTED

DEUTERONOMY 4:44–6:25

I've had the privilege of visiting Washington D. C. many times. On my last visit, I was reminded of the overwhelming evidence of the influence of the Bible on the founding of our nation.

Walking through the enormous Library of Congress, I looked up and read these words of Tennyson inscribed above a large column: "One God, one law, one element, and one far-off divine event, to which the whole creation moves."

As I walked up to the front steps of the U. S. Supreme Court, I gazed up to see what is perhaps the most visible evidence of the Bible's influence on our nation. In the center of the frieze above the main entrance, Moses is holding the two tablets of the Ten Commandments.

The Ten Commandments are so important that Moses chose this opportunity in Deuteronomy to repeat them to a new generation that hadn't heard the voice of God thundering from Mount Sinai. More than mere laws for living, the Ten Commandments are actually 10 wonderful facets of God's character.

HONOR GOD FIRST (DEUT. 5:6-7)

In the first commandment, God revealed His character by revealing His name. The original Hebrew language spelled God's name with these four consonants, YHWH. There are no vowels in the original Hebrew, only 22 consonants. Modern Hebrew has added vowel points to aid in pronunciation, but translators can only guess what the vowel sounds were like. These four consonants, YHWH (called the "Tetragrammaton"), appear more than 6,000 times in the Old Testament.

The name of God was so holy that the Jews would never speak it aloud because they were afraid they might pronounce it incorrectly, which would constitute blasphemy. Since they refused to pronounce YHWH, they substituted another Hebrew word, *Adonai,* which means, "Lord." Anytime we see the English word "Lord" in the Old Testament, it is actually YHWH.

The most important discovery you'll ever make in your life is that God exists. The second most important discovery you'll make is that you can know Him.

In 1492, Columbus sailed westward from Europe looking for India. When he got to the Caribbean he named the islands the West Indies, and he called the people he found "Indians." He returned to Spain and declared, "I have discovered a new world." Columbus didn't invent it or create it because it had been there all along. He just stumbled onto it.

The same is true with knowing God. We did not invent or initiate that relationship. God will not force you to have fellowship with Him, but He loves you and He desires to have a relationship with you. Each of us must make this personal discovery for ourselves.

How do you personally demonstrate reverence for a holy God in your daily life?

What is the difference between Christianity as a religion and Christianity as a relationship?

» LEARNING ACTIVITY

A GOD OF MANY NAMES

Throughout the Bible, the writers described their personal interaction with God to reflect His specific characteristics. Match the following names of God in Scripture with their meaning:

___ 1. El Shaddai (Gen. 17:1)	a. The Lord is my shepherd
___ 2. El Elyon (Gen. 14:20)	b. The Almighty God
___ 3. Adonai (Gen. 15:2)	c. The LORD will provide
___ 4. Jehovah Rohi (Raah) (Ps. 23)	d. The Everlasting God
___ 5. Jehovah Rapha (Ex. 15:26)	e. Lord/Master
___ 6. Jehovah Shalom (Judg. 6:24)	f. God/Creator
___ 7. Immanuel (Isa. 7:14)	g. The Lord who heals
___ 8. Elohim (Gen. 1:1)	h. The Most High God
___ 9. Jehovah Jireh (Gen. 22:14)	i. God with us
___ 10. El Olam (Gen. 21:33)	j. The Lord is peace

What are some of your favorite names for God? Why?

Answers: 1-b, 2-h, 3-e, 4-a, 5-g, 6-j, 7-i, 8-f, 9-c, 10-d

KEEP YOUR WORSHIP REAL (DEUT. 5:8-10)

Have you ever seen a poster or a television program about Mount Rushmore in South Dakota? No television screen, poster, or even wide screen movie can capture the majesty and beauty of that massive sculpture. The four faces of George Washington, Thomas Jefferson, Abraham Lincoln, and Theodore Roosevelt have been chiseled into the side of Mount Rushmore. Each face is almost 100 feet tall. Any image (or picture) of Mount Rushmore only reduces it. Seeing it in person is the only way to experience its wonder and majesty.

What if I gave you a handful of clay and asked you to make a representation of Mount Rushmore? You might try, but you would not be able to come close to demonstrating its greatness. Your little clay replica would actually be an insult to the real thing—no matter how many they sold in the souvenir shops.

That's exactly why God forbids worship of any "image." No material image can truly represent Him, and any attempt

Below: Mount Rushmore
ISTOCK PHOTO

to do so actually insults His greatness. To put it simply, a material image is just a bad picture of God.

You could probably do a better job describing Rushmore using only your words. Those listening to you could let their imagination envision it bigger than any picture you could show them. We often use the expression, "A picture is worth a thousand words." However, when it comes to the nature of God, He has chosen to use thousands of words (the Bible) rather than any one picture.

The primary danger of using material images in worship is that these images may come to represent God instead of reminding us of God. The Bible does not forbid symbols, but it does forbid idols. What is the difference? A symbol reminds us of God, but an idol or an image may be used to represent God. When we cross over the line to something that represents God, instead of just reminding us of God, we've entered into the sin of idolatry.

When you picture what God looks like, what do you see?

Where do you see examples of modern day idolatry?

BE CAREFUL WITH YOUR WORDS (DEUT. 5:11)

In the Bible, God's character is linked to His name. In our American culture, names don't really demonstrate character. We use names only to identify people. The federal government knows us as a taxpayer ID number. The state knows us by our driver's license number. We might as well be a number because a number actually does a better job of identifying us. Others may share our name, but not our Social Security number. We just use names as convenient labels.

In Bible times, every name carried a message. Names were more than just numbers to distinguish and identify people; they said something about the person. Jacob and Esau were twin sons born to Isaac and Rebecca. Esau, the firstborn, was covered with red hair, so he was given a name that means "hairy." Jacob was born holding on to the heel of his older brother, so his parents gave him a name which means "grabber." That name came to describe the personality of Jacob because for much of his life, he was a grabber. He grabbed for things that were not rightfully his. He grabbed for Esau's birthright. Later, when he had a wrestling encounter with an angel, he grabbed onto the angel and wouldn't let him go. God said, "No longer is your name Grabber. Because your character will change, your name must change." God gave Jacob a new name that represented his transformed character—Israel, which means "prince of God."

Today, God's name is insulted regularly. Vulgar profanity has become a normal part of our national conversation. To insult His holy name is to insult His character. Taking the Lord's name in vain is more than speaking God's name joined with an expletive. Whenever you use God's name in an empty, meaningless fashion, you are actually violating this commandment. How many empty prayers have we uttered in the Lord's name? How many empty songs about the Lord have we sung?

To insult His holy name is to insult His character.

Even though this is a negative command, I prefer to look for the positive side. God is inviting us to honor His name, respect His name, and exalt His name.

In the Old Testament, God revealed His name as YHWH. However, we can know Him by a new name. Romans 10:13 says, "For everyone who calls on the name of the Lord will be saved." Notice it doesn't say, "For everyone who calls on the Lord will be saved." You must call on the *name* of the Lord to be saved. You often hear many people talk about "the Good Lord" or "the Man Upstairs." It isn't "the Good Lord" who will save you; nor is it "the Man Upstairs." The Lord has a name and His name is Jesus. In Acts 4:12 we read, "There is salvation in no one else, for there is no other name under heaven given to people, and we must be saved by it." Jesus is the only name that will get you into heaven. Don't take that name lightly.

Jesus is the only name that will get you into heaven. Don't take that name lightly.

Why is our culture so casual about the name of God?

What can you do to avoid using God's name in an empty, meaningless way?

TAKE TIME TO REST (DEUT. 5:12-15)

I've been in Jerusalem many times on a Friday afternoon. For the Jews, their Sabbath begins at sundown on Friday and lasts until sunset on Saturday. It is both amazing and refreshing to see the transformation that occurs in Jerusalem when the Sabbath begins. A curtain of serenity, tranquility, and quietness falls over the Jewish part of this holy city. The hectic noise of busses, trucks, and cars is replaced by silence on most of the streets. An eerie stillness replaces the constant drone of construction. And all of this happens in the more secular sections of Jerusalem.

Christians are confused about how the Sabbath law should be observed today. Does this commandment forbid the opening of retail stores on Sunday? Should we go to football games, play golf, or go fishing on Sunday?

You can find the other nine commandments repeated somewhere in the New Testament—but not the Sabbath Commandment. The Sabbath wasn't given to the church; it was give to the nation of Israel. God said, "Tell the Israelites: You must observe My Sabbaths, for it is a sign between Me and you throughout your generations" (Ex. 31:13a).

The New Testament reveals that Christians are not bound by the Jewish Sabbath law. In Colossians 2:14-17, the apostle Paul wrote about the impact of Jesus' death. "He erased the certificate of debt, with its obligations, that was against us and opposed to us, and has taken it out of the way by nailing it to the cross ... Therefore, don't let anyone judge you in regard to food and drink or in the matter of a festival or a new moon or a Sabbath day. These are a shadow of what was to come; the substance is the Messiah."

Whereas the fourth commandment is not an immutable moral law of God, it is a biblical principle that New Testament Christians should observe. The New Testament teaches that it is good to work, but the spirit of the fourth commandment teaches that if all you ever do is work, you will be missing God's best for your life. Everyone needs to work, but everyone also needs to rest (Sabbath) or they will soon be overcome with weariness. Taking one day in seven to rest serves the purpose of renewing your strength and gives you time to focus on God.

Sabbath means "rest." Jesus is the Lord of the Sabbath, and He is our Sabbath. He issued this invitation to us, "Come to Me, all of you who are weary and burdened, and I will give you rest. All of you, take up My yoke and learn from Me, because I am gentle and humble in heart, and you will find rest for yourselves. For My yoke is easy and My burden is light" (Matt. 11:28-30). Jesus can be your true Sabbath seven days a week.

What does the Sabbath mean to you?

How can a Christian achieve balance between work and rest?

HONOR YOUR PARENTS (DEUT. 5:16)

The fifth commandment is the pivotal commandment. The first four commandments address our relationship with God. The last six commandments address our human relationships. The arrangement of these commandments is not accidental. We must be in a right relationship with God before we can relate correctly to those around us.

The Hebrew word for "honor" is *kabed,* which means "to lend weight or dignity toward." Whether you are a child living at home or even an adult with one or more living parents, this command is still in force. We never grow out of the moral obligation that God has given us.

As we age, we move through periods of transitions with our parents. As children, our primary focus is to *obey* them. As teenagers, our requirement is to *respect* them. As we age, and our parents grow older, our responsibility is to *treasure* them.

You may have a problem with honoring your parents because you have parents who didn't treat you well. Perhaps you have been the victim of verbal, physical, or sexual abuse. Maybe you are angry with your mom or dad because they divorced, mistreated you, or failed to show the kind of love you think you deserved. How can you honor them if this is the case? First, admit there is a problem. If possible, in a loving way, communicate those feelings to your parents. Don't let another week go by without addressing the issue. Express your frustrations and feelings with them. Then, forgive your parents and ask them to forgive you for not treasuring them the way you should. The last years of your relationship can be the best.

Hidden below the surface of the fifth commandment is a principle for parents. Your responsibility is that you must be honorable. Your goal should be to live as the kind of parent that your children can honor. The very best thing that parents can give their children is a good example of what is right and what is wrong.

Parents, you can tell your kids to pray, but unless they see that prayer is important to you, chances are they are not going to pray much. You can tell them to read the Bible, but unless they observe you studying the Word, they are not going to read it much.

How can you be a better Christian model for your children (or younger generations if you don't have children)?

Why is it important for parents to earn the respect of their children?

VALUE THE SANCTITY OF LIFE (DEUT. 5:17)

Some people believe that this commandment forbids killing of any kind. They believe that it is wrong to kill a bug, or a deer, or a fish, or an enemy soldier. The King James Version reads, "Thou shalt not kill." The word for "kill" is the Hebrew word *ratsach,* which is correctly translated "murder" in the Holman Christian Standard Bible. This refers to one individual taking the life of another because of personal anger or hostility toward that person.

Another symptom of America's moral decay is the prevalence of violence and murder. America leads the civilized world in our level of violence. Someone is murdered in America every eight minutes. While you are reading this chapter, four Americans will become the victim of homicide. Jesus taught that the anger and hatred that motivates murder comes from a sinful heart. He said, "For from within, out of people's hearts, come evil thoughts, sexual immoralities, thefts, murders" (Mark 7:21).

But infanticide is much more prevalent in America than homicide. This includes both the killing of a newborn infant or a pre-born infant. Without question, abortion is America's worst violation of the sixth commandment. How has our culture become so insensitive to the value of life that we can sanction the medical removal of a child from his or her mother's womb?

More than a million abortions are performed in America every year. We are facing a moral crisis. As Christian citizens we must speak the truth in love that abortion is a horrible violation of the sixth commandment.

What does "sanctity of life" mean to you?

What can you do to "speak the truth in love" about abortion?

BE FAITHFUL TO YOUR MATE (DEUT. 5:18)

Simply stated, adultery is any sex outside the marriage relationship. If you aren't married, you may be thinking, "I can't violate the seventh commandment because I am single." The Hebrew word for adultery is *na'aph,* which means "sexual sin" outside of marriage. If you are single, premarital sex violates this command. If you are married, you violate the seventh commandment by having extramarital sex. Any sexual behavior outside the bonds of marriage is a violation of the seventh commandment.

Why does God speak so candidly about sexual purity? It's because God created each of us with a powerful sex drive. Sex was not something that we dreamed up; it is a gift from God. In God's eyes, sex between a husband and wife is holy and pure. God created sex for two purposes: to enable a husband and wife to express intimate affection with each other and to populate the earth. Your sex drive is not something that should make you feel ashamed—it should be enjoyed—but only in the confines of marriage. Any other use of sex is an abuse of sex.

Adultery can also be committed through sexual fantasy. Even if you have never been physically involved outside your marriage, Jesus said you could violate this commandment in your mind and in your heart if you fantasize about a sexual relationship with someone who is not your spouse (Matt. 5:28). Is it wrong to look at another person and think that he or she is attractive? No, that's normal.

To have a tempting thought is not sin—but to entertain that thought is to cross over into sin.

Martin Luther said, "You can't help it if a bird flies over your head, but you don't need to let him make a nest in your hair." The same is true about tempting thoughts. To have a tempting thought is not sin, but to entertain that thought is to cross over into sin. The first look at an attractive person usually is not sin, but the second, third, and fourth look can become sin. Sexual fantasy often leads to sexual sin. It is only a short step on a slippery slope to graduate from fantasizing about somebody to enacting that fantasy.

Why is it important to ask God's help in controlling your thoughts?

How has our culture abused the meaning of human sexuality?

RESPECT THE PROPERTY OF OTHERS (DEUT. 5:19)

One reason people steal is simply that they are greedy and selfish. They just want more and more of something—money, property, or anything else that can be stolen. The sinful human nature says in effect, "I'm going to take what I do not have. It's not right for someone else to have so much, so I will correct this imbalance." The Bible speaks to that very clearly in Ephesians 4:28, "The thief must no longer steal. Instead, he must do honest work with his own hands, so that he has something to share with anyone in need." The antidote for theft is hard work.

There are two legitimate ways that you can obtain goods or money. You can work for it, or you may receive it as a gift. Any other way of obtaining possessions is outside the will of God. When you think about robbery, you may picture a hold-up at a bank or store. But stealing minor items from work or a friend's house also violates this commandment. It is not the amount being stolen that makes one a thief—but the act itself. Stealing violates a fundamental human right that God has given us—the right to have private property. Basic human dignity is tied up in the right to private property.

Proverbs 11:1 says, "Dishonest scales are detestable to the LORD, but an accurate weight is His delight." In Bible times, there were merchants who were cheating their customers by using scales that were dishonest. Today, white-collar crime is even more sophisticated and includes computer/Internet fraud, credit card fraud, telemarketing fraud, money laundering, tax evasion, mail fraud, and insider trading. Whether it is cheating in school, cheating in business, being deceptive about an expense report, or trying to get more out of your customers than you ought, it is fraud and a violation of the eighth commandment.

Where do you see this commandment being abused in our culture today?

What can you do protect yourself from the temptation to obtain possessions outside the will of God?

HONESTY IS THE ONLY POLICY (DEUT. 5:20)

God hates words that deceive. Before you choke on the word "hate," consider these words from Proverbs: "The LORD hates six things; in fact, seven are detestable to Him: arrogant eyes, a lying tongue, hands that shed innocent blood, a heart that plots wicked schemes, feet eager to run to evil, a lying witness who gives false testimony, and one who stirs up trouble among brothers" (Prov. 6:16-19). Of the seven things listed that God hates, two of them have to do with the ninth commandment. The very character of God is that of truth. Any kind of deception or lie is an insult to His truthful character.

The Bible says in Psalm 58:3, "The wicked go astray from the womb; liars err from birth." Parents don't have to teach their children to lie; they just come by it naturally. Rather, children must be taught to tell the truth. At one time (or perhaps many times), all of us have told a lie, practiced deception, or used exaggerations or embellishment. It takes only one lie to make a liar. Every lie offends God because it is a violation of His character of truth.

In the story of Pinocchio, his nose grew longer every time he told a lie. That effect, though embarrassing, was actually a gift in disguise. Pinocchio (and everyone else) knew immediately when a lie had been told. Have you ever wished you had an internal bell or buzzer that would go off every time you lied or used an exaggeration? You do have a resource like that—He is called the indwelling Holy Spirit of God. Jesus called Him "the Spirit of truth" (John 15:26). When you speak or live a lie, the Holy Spirit in you will warn you. If you are a Christian, you have to deny or suppress the "Spirit of truth" every time you tell a lie.

What are some of the damaging consequences of lying to others?

What can you do to guard against the temptation to exaggerate, embellish, or outright lie to others?

LEARN TO LIVE WITH CONTENTMENT (DEUT. 5:21)

The word "covet" is the Hebrew word *chamad,* which means to "have an intense desire" for something. Actually, there's nothing wrong with coveting—if you covet the proper thing. I might say to you, "I covet your prayers." There's certainly nothing wrong with that. It is the object of our covetousness that makes certain desires a sin.

It seems as if we're are all trying to "keep up with the Joneses." When we see our neighbor with more "stuff" than we have, it makes us want to have at least as much as they have. If they get a new car, we feel we need a new car, too. If we see a new big-screen television being delivered to their house, we start scheming how we can get one.

Covetousness (greed) makes a person a victim of a vicious cycle of dissatisfaction. If your goal in life is to get more things and to accumulate possessions, you will never be satisfied. If you get a new car, before long it gets a little dull or scratched, and you start noticing all the newer and shinier models on the street. You assumed that your new automobile would satisfy for a while, but it didn't. You buy a new home and think it is so wonderful, but you'll soon start noticing that there is always another house that is bigger and better than yours. If "having the best" becomes the primary source of satisfaction in your life, you are cursed because you never will be satisfied.

The cure for covetousness is contentment in Christ. Contentment means being satisfied with what you have. The Bible says, "Your life should be free from the love of money. Be satisfied with what you have, for He Himself has said, 'I will never leave you or forsake you'" (Heb. 13:5).

The cure for covetousness is contentment in Christ.

What is your definition of personal "contentment"?

What does it mean to be content in Christ?

Moses concluded this oration by saying, "Love the Lord your God with all your heart, with all your soul, and with all your strength" (Deut. 6:5).

In Matthew 22 an expert in the Law asked Jesus to identify the greatest commandment. Jesus answered by quoting Deuteronomy 6:5. He added that the second commandment was to "love your neighbor as yourself," which is found in Leviticus 19:18.

When you truly love God, you won't violate the first four commandments. Likewise, when you sincerely love your neighbor, you won't have to worry about keeping the last six commandments.

Will you pause right now and ask God to give you the strength to love Him more dearly?

Will you ask Him to give you a deeper love for your neighbor?

A CLOSER LOOK

The Mezuzah

In the homes and hotel rooms in Israel you'll find a little rectangular box affixed to the doorpost. This little box is called a mezuzah, it contains the Scripture found in Deuteronomy 6:4-9. If you visit my home in Tyler, Texas you'll see a mezuzah on our front doorpost. The Jews literally obey the command to keep God's Word on their doorposts. As followers of Jesus we joyfully affix God's Word to the doorposts of our hearts.

How can you spend more time in God's Word this week?

» LEARNING ACTIVITY

IN OUR HOMES

Deuteronomy 6:4-9 is known as The Shema—a transliteration of the Hebrew imperative meaning "hear" (Deut. 6:4). These verses are recognized as the basic statement of the Jewish Law. The Shema is described as "a confession of faith by which they acknowledged the one true God and His commandments for them." When Jesus was asked about the "greatest commandment," He answered by quoting from the Shema (Mark 12:29).

In the space provided, list some specific, practical ways you can practice each portion of verses 5-9.

"Love the LORD your God will all your heart, with all your soul, and with all your strength" (v. 5).

"These words that I am giving you today are to be in your heart" (v. 6).

"Repeat them to your children. Talk about them when you sit in your house and when you walk along the road, when you lie down and when you get up" (v. 7).

"Bind them as a sign on your hand and let them be a symbol on your forehead. Write them on the doorposts of your house and on your gates." (vv. 8-9).

CHAPTER 3

GOD'S PEOPLE SEPARATED

DEUTERONOMY 7:1–10:11

As Generation 2.0 approached Canaan, God required that they remain holy. They would be entering a country where the customs and cultures were different. They must remain holy by refusing to embrace those pagan customs and cultures.

I like to fish, but I'm not very good at it. A few years ago, a rancher in our church invited me to come out and fish in his tank. For non-Texans, a tank is what most other people call a farm-pond. He had an old aluminum boat he kept on shore, and he told me I was welcome to use it anytime. I wanted to spend some quality time with my younger daughter, so I offered to take her fishing. We drove out to the ranch and loaded our meager fishing gear and a sack lunch into the boat. I shoved off from the shore and started paddling out toward the center of the small tank.

After a few minutes my daughter said to me, "Uh, dad. I think we've got a problem."

I looked down and the bottom of the boat was quickly filling with water. I had forgotten to put the plug into the drain hole in the stern of the boat. By now, the water was too deep to find the plug, and we didn't have anything to bail out the water. I quickly started rowing back to the shore, but the boat became too heavy. I had to jump out into the waist-deep water and drag the water-filled boat to shore.

We were both wet, and our sack lunch was ruined. I finally manhandled the boat on shore and turned it so that the water could drain out the hole in the stern. We loaded up and headed home, then we stopped at Whataburger® for lunch.

We have been sent into the world,
but we must not allow the world to get in us.

A boat does great when it's in the water. But if the water gets in the boat, a fishing trip can be ruined. The same is true when it comes to our relationship with the world. We have been sent into the world, but we must not allow the world to get in us.

What are some ways that the "world" slowly gets "in our boat"?

What does it mean to be in the world, but not of it? (See John 17:15-16.)

» LEARNING ACTIVITY

CALLED TO BE DIFFERENT

As God led His people into Canaan, He called them to live different lives from the people they would encounter. For each of the areas listed below, identify a cultural influence that presents a challenge to holiness today.

Speech

Media choices

Purity

Marriage

GOD HAS CHOSEN US TO BE DIFFERENT (DEUT. 7:1-11)

Moses told the Canaan-bound congregation, "For you are a holy people belonging to the Lord your God. The LORD your God has chosen you to be His own possession out of all the peoples on the face of the earth" (7:6). We use the word *holy* in many contexts. In our culture it almost has become a term of derision. People describe certain Christians as "holy rollers," or they speak of someone feeling as if they are "holier than thou."

In its most basic meaning, the word *holy* means "different." It could also be understood as "one-of-a-kind" or "out-of-the-ordinary." For instance, the word *Bible* literally means "book." But what makes the Bible different is that it is the "Holy Bible." It is different than any other book written in the history of the world.

When Isaiah fell on his face before God in Isaiah 6, the seraphim were chanting, "Holy, holy, holy is the LORD of Hosts" (v. 3) There were many false gods, but the One True Living God was "different" than any other—that made Him holy.

The children of Israel were "holy." That means they were "different" than any other nation or tribe. In His grace, God had chosen them out of all the nations of the earth. The word *special* is so overused that it has lost its meaning, but the Jews really were special among all the people of the earth.

They were about to enter a land that had different cultures, customs, and languages. God warned them against being assimilated into the godless culture. Instead they had to maintain their unique relationship with Yahweh.

But God didn't choose them because they were superior to all the people of the earth. Instead God chose them to be a blessing to all the other nations. When God first called Abram He said, "I will bless those who bless you, I will curse those who treat you with contempt, and all the peoples on earth will be blessed through you" (Gen. 12:3).

As followers of Jesus Christ, we are called to be holy. We should be "out-of-the-ordinary" individuals. Our culture doesn't embrace a biblical worldview, so we are called to be different. The apostle Peter wrote, "Be holy, because I am holy" (1 Pet. 1:16).

We should be "out-of-the-ordinary" individuals.

When people examine your conduct and vocabulary, what are the noticeable differences between your lifestyle and those who don't claim to be followers of Jesus Christ?

How does it make you feel to consider yourself "holy"?

GOD KEEPS HIS PROMISES (DEUT. 7:12-16)

Our God is a covenant-making Lord. He made a covenant with Noah and gave the sign of a rainbow to seal the covenant. He made a covenant with Abraham, and circumcision was the sign. He made a covenant with Moses; the Law, written by His finger, was His signature.

God always keeps His covenants. The parties with whom He makes a covenant do not always keep their part.

God is the original promise keeper. According to Dr. Herbert Lockyer, who wrote *All the Promises in the Bible,* there are 3,573 promises in the Bible.

Moses communicated God's amazing promise to this generation of Israelites. He said, "If you listen to and are careful to keep these ordinances, the Lord your God will keep His covenant loyalty with you, as He swore to your fathers. He will love you, bless you, and multiply you. He will bless your descendants, and the produce of your land—your grain, new wine, and oil—the young of your herds, and the newborn of your flocks, in the land He swore to your fathers that He would give you" (7:12-13).

God made a three-fold promise with this generation. He promised to love them, bless them, and to multiply them. It is His love that motivates His blessing. The manifestation of His blessing was seen in the multiplication of children, flocks, and fields.

God has also made a covenant with us—it's His new covenant that Jesus established by His death. On the night before He went to the cross, Jesus announced this covenant: "As they were eating, Jesus took bread, blessed and broke it, gave it to the disciples, and said, 'Take and eat it; this is My body.' Then He took a cup, and after giving thanks, He gave it to them and said, 'Drink from it, all of you. For this is My blood that establishes the covenant; it is shed for many for the forgiveness of sins'" (Matt. 26:26-28).

God's promises to us will never fail. Paul wrote, "For every one of God's promises is 'Yes' in Him. Therefore, the 'Amen' is also spoken through Him by us for God's glory" (2 Cor. 1:20).

All of us have heard promises that were broken. When you hear a person say, "I promise," we take it with a grain of salt. In this life you'll hear empty promises like, "This will only take a moment of your time;" "I'm not trying to sell you anything;" "This won't hurt a bit;" or "If I'm elected I will ...." As much as we like to keep our promises, sometimes we fail.

All of God's promises are in Christ, and they are rock solid.

But all of God's promises are in Christ, and they are rock solid. He says, "Yes! I love you unconditionally—I promise in Christ. Yes! I can forgive all your sins—I promise in Christ. Yes! I have a wonderful plan for your life—I promise in Christ!"

Which of God's promises have been particularly meaningful to you lately? Why?

How do you know that God's promises are completely trustworthy?

GOD IS MIGHTIER THAN YOUR ENEMIES (DEUT. 7:17-26)

In the 1980 Winter Olympics at Lake Placid, New York, the U.S. Hockey team faced the stronger and faster Soviet team. The Soviets had won the world hockey championship since 1954. They were considered unbeatable. They were active-duty military officers who practiced year round in a world-class facility. A year earlier this same Soviet team had defeated the NHL all-stars 6-0.

On the other hand, the U.S. team consisted of a mixture of amateur and college hockey players. Everyone expected the Soviet team to trounce the U.S. team. But if you've seen the movie *Miracle on Ice* you know the outcome.

U.S. Coach Herb Brooks convinced the underdog American team that they could pull off the upset. He convinced them to play their game as a team rather than a group of superstars. As the final seconds wound down with the U.S. team leading 4-3, sportscaster Al Michaels shouted, "Do you believe in miracles?"

In the conquest of Canaan, the Israelites were the military underdogs. And the only way they could conquer the Canaanite nations would be through a miracle from God. The people of God were facing some of the strongest armies on the earth. Jericho was the most heavily fortified city of the ancient world. There were still giants in the land. It would have been easy to give in to fear. Moses, their head coach, encouraged them. But he didn't tell them to trust in their own abilities; he charged them to trust in the power of their God. He said, "Don't be terrified of them, for the LORD your God, a great and awesome God, is among you" (7:21).

There are times when each of us faces frightful enemies who try to make us afraid. Your enemy might be called cancer, grief, heartache, or rejection. The Lord Jesus told His disciples, "Don't fear those who kill the body, and after that can do nothing more ... Aren't five sparrows sold for two pennies? Yet not one of them is forgotten in God's sight. Indeed, the hairs of your head are all counted. Don't be afraid; you are worth more than many sparrows!" (Luke 12:4,6-7).

God cares so much for each of us that He has numbered the hairs on our head. For some of us going bald, we've made His job easier! But the point is that God cares about the tiniest details of our lives. When it comes to His compassion for us, nothing is trivial to our Creator.

» LEARNING ACTIVITY

GOD IS STRONGER

How would you complete this acrostic to describe how God is stronger than any enemy you might face?

S
T
R
O
N
G
E
R

A pastor friend of mine taught me that a good acrostic for FEAR is "False Evidence Appearing Real." When we look at things from our earthly perspective, those gigantic enemies appear to be unbeatable. But when we look at them from the perspective of God, they seem tiny compared to His power.

The next time you're facing enemies that seem to be stronger than you, just claim this promise: God is mightier than your enemies.

When was a time you faced a problem that seemed larger-than-life and God helped you?

How can you remind yourself to rely on God to help you whenever you face troubles?

GOD WILL MEET YOUR NEEDS (DEUT. 8:1-10)

For much of my life when I read about the children of Israel wandering in the wilderness, I imagined a thick forest—like the wilderness of the Rocky Mountains. But when I first visited the Judean Wilderness, I was in for a shock. I saw some of the most barren land on the planet. The wilderness is basically an inhospitable desert with steep hills and ravines. I saw a few scraggly scrubs dotting the landscape. I wondered how anyone could survive there with no food and water.

The only way the Israelites survived the wilderness was because a loving God provided manna from heaven and water from a rock. Moses reminded the people, "He humbled you by letting you go hungry; then He gave you manna to eat, which you and your fathers had not known" (8:3).

It's mind-boggling to consider the massive amount of manna that God provided for two million people over a 40-year period. Each family was instructed to pick up an omer daily (Ex. 16:16), which was approximately two quarts. When you extrapolate that amount for 600,000 families over 40 years, that means that God provided approximately nine billion gallons of manna! How could He do that? Simple. There's no shortage in heaven.

Moses reminded the Israelites again how compassionate and caring the Lord had been to them during their 40 years in the wilderness. He said, "Your clothing did not wear out, and your feet did not swell these 40 years" (Deut. 8:4). Do you have any clothes in your closet that are 40 years old? Chances are, you don't—especially if you wore them every day. Do you have a pair of shoes that haven't worn out after 40 years of wearing them? Probably not.

The same God who took care of the Israelites in the wilderness has promised to meet your needs as well. "And my God will supply all your needs according to His riches in glory in Christ Jesus" (Phil. 4:19).

We often mistake "needs" with "wants." If you have enough food to eat, enough clothes to stay warm, and a roof over your head, then your needs are being met. In fact, compared to most of the world's population we are rich. My definition of rich is "having all your needs met, and having the capacity to enjoy life."

We often mistake "needs" with "wants."

What is your definition of being "rich"?

When was a time you experienced God's miraculous provision?

GOD GIVES YOU THE ABILITY TO PRODUCE (DEUT. 8:11-20)

George Truett, the legendary pastor of First Baptist Church, Dallas, once visited a wealthy rancher in West Texas. The rancher was proud of what he had built. He owned thousands of acres of land, some with producing oil wells. He owned thousands of head of cattle. In the middle of his personal empire he constructed a magnificent mansion. It was four stories tall, contained an elevator, and had a large porch on the top, from which the tycoon could survey his kingdom.

After sharing dinner with Dr. Truett, the rancher invited him up to the top of the ranch house. He pointed south toward the cattle fields and said, "Preacher, I own everything in that direction as far you can see." Then he pointed north toward a man-made lake he had built. He said, "Preacher, I own everything in that direction as far as you can see." He turned left and pointed west over the cultivated cotton fields. "And I own everything in that direction as far as you can see." He turned around and pointed at his working oil derricks, and said, "And preacher, I own everything in that direction as far as you can see." Dr. Truett was silent for a few minutes, and then he pointed a finger toward heaven and said, "But, sir, how much do you own in *that* direction?"

Perhaps you know someone who takes great pride in the wealth they've accumulated over a lifetime of hard work. You might even be someone like that. Be careful that you don't take too much credit. Hidden here in this amazing Book of Deuteronomy is one of the most powerful principles in all of God's Word.

Moses sounds like he was speaking to 21st-century Americans when he said,

> When you eat and are full, and build beautiful houses to live in, and your herds and flocks grow large, and your silver and gold multiply, and everything else you have increases, be careful that your heart doesn't become proud and you forget the LORD your God who brought you out of the land of Egypt, ... You may say to yourself, "My power and my own ability have gained this wealth for me," but remember that the LORD your God gives you the power to gain wealth (8:12-14,17-18).

What is the balance between utilizing your gifts and talents and giving God credit for your success?

How can you give God more of the credit for your accomplishments so He gets all of the glory?

GOD CALLS US TO SERVE HIM (DEUT. 9:1–10:11)

God had Moses set apart the tribe of Levi for priestly duties. "At that time the LORD set apart the tribe of Levi to carry the ark of the LORD's covenant, to stand before Yahweh to serve Him, and to pronounce blessings in His name, as it is today" (10:8).

The role of a priest is to serve the Lord by serving those who worship the Lord. A priest talks to God on behalf of the people—that's prayer. And a priest talks to the people on behalf of God—that's preaching.

Although the priesthood was reserved for a single tribe during the time of Moses, today, all of God's people are priests. The apostle Peter expressed it this way, "But you are a chosen race, a royal priesthood, a holy nation, a people for His possession, so that you may proclaim the praises of the One who called you out of darkness into His marvelous light" (1 Pet. 2:9).

We embrace the wonderful principle of the priesthood of all believers. That means that there is no spiritual hierarchy in the church. We are all servants of the Lord.

In what ways are you carrying out your "priestly" duties?

A CLOSER LOOK

The Power of God's Word

After Jesus' baptism, the Spirit led Him into the wilderness where He fasted for 40 days. Afterwards, Satan came to tempt Jesus. He challenged a weakened, starving man to prove His power by turning stones into bread. Having walked those wilderness trails myself, I can affirm that many of the large rocks have the shape and size of a nice loaf of bread. But instead of giving in to the Devil's temptation, Jesus quoted Deuteronomy 8:3. Jesus said, "It is written: 'Man must not live on bread alone but on every word that comes from the mouth of God'" (Matt. 4:4).

In each of the three temptations, Jesus defeated Satan by quoting a Scripture from Deuteronomy. Jesus could have easily disposed of the Devil with His supernatural power. But instead He defeated Satan by quoting three short Scriptures. That's a powerful reminder to us that quoting Scripture when we face temptation is a great deterrent to sin. The benefit of memorizing God's Word is that it keeps us from sin. The psalmist sang, "I have treasured Your word in my heart so that I may not sin against You" (Ps. 119:11). Jesus resisted the Devil with three obscure verses from Deuteronomy; just think, we have access to Romans, John, and Revelation and all of the Bible to quote in the Devil's face!

How can you prioritize memorizing more of God's Word?

How can you use God's Word in everyday temptations?

CHAPTER 4

GOD'S CHARACTER DEMONSTRATED IN WORSHIP

DEUTERONOMY 10:12–18:22

I once had church member make a statement like this to me: "I believe in the God of love found in the New Testament; but I don't like the God of wrath found in the Old Testament." I politely pointed out that there is only one God, and that the God of the Old Testament is the same God found in the New Testament. I even showed him where God said, "Because I, Yahweh, have not changed, you descendants of Jacob have not been destroyed" (Mal. 3:6).

This man missed the point that both the Old and New Testaments reveal a God of love and compassion. He loves His people enough to clearly reveal how they may walk in fellowship with Him.

GOD IS COMPASSIONATE AND LOVING (DEUT. 10:12-22)

As Moses instructed the people, he inserted many references to the love of God. He said,

> The heavens, indeed the highest heavens, belong to the LORD your God, as does the earth and everything in it. Yet the LORD was devoted to your fathers and loved them. He chose their descendants after them—He chose you out of all the peoples, as it is today (Deut. 10:14-15).

God created the people of every nation, but in His grace, He chose the Israelites for a special purpose—to spread His name among the other nations. Years later, when the Jewish nation grew stronger and conquered their enemies, they forgot that God chose them for this purpose. At the height of their military and economic power under David and Solomon, the Israelites imagined that God loved them more than the other nations.

But even before they entered Canaan, God reminded the people that His love is directed to all people, not just the Jews.

> For the LORD your God is the God of gods and Lord of lords, the great, mighty, and awesome God, showing no partiality and taking no bribe. He executes justice for the fatherless and the widow, and loves the foreigner, giving him food and clothing. You also must love the foreigner, since you were foreigners in the land of Egypt (10:17-19).

Most of us who live in America believe it is the greatest nation in the world. We realize that God has blessed us. But we must avoid the mistake of thinking we have "favored status" with God. God loves every person on the planet. Because He loves them, we should love them enough to tell them the good news that God loves them.

» LEARNING ACTIVITY

WHAT GOD REQUIRES

In Deuteronomy 10:12-13, Moses outlined several basic requirements for God's people as they prepared to enter the promised land.

• "fear the LORD your God by walking in all His ways" (v. 12)
How are you demonstrating a reverence for the Lord in the way you conduct yourself each day?

• "love Him" (v. 12)
How do you express your love for God?

• "worship the LORD your God with all your heart and all your soul" (v. 12)
To what degree are you actively engaged in personal and corporate worship?

• "Keep the LORD's commands and statues" (v. 13)
How well are you living in obedience to God's commands and teachings?

GOD WILL BLESS YOUR CROPS (DEUT. 11:1-12)

Every spring and summer, my wife and I plant a vegetable garden. We have four raised beds; each one is twelve feet long and six feet wide. We grow pole beans, cucumbers, eggplant, tomatoes, and a variety of peppers.

My wife has a green thumb, and she says I have a black thumb. So she's the main gardener and I'm "the help." I clean out the garden and till it for the next crop. She does all the planting and cultivating. I help with the picking, and of course, my favorite part is the eating. It takes a lot of hard work and time to bring in a crop.

The people of Israel were moving into a land where they would have to raise crops. The manna that God had been providing for 40 years was about to cease. This generation of Israelites knew little about agriculture because nomads are never still long enough to harvest food—plus the wilderness was not fertile. Even so, God cared enough for them to promise to bless their crops. He said,

> For the land you are entering to possess is not like the land of Egypt, from which you have come, where you sowed your seed and irrigated by hand as in a vegetable garden. But the land you are entering to possess is a land of mountains and valleys, watered by rain from the sky. It is a land the LORD your God cares for. He is always watching over it from the beginning to the end of the year (11:10-12).

Agriculture in Egypt consisted of transporting water from the Nile to the place where the gardens were located. But God was taking them into a land where He would personally watch over their gardens and send them rain.

When I was in high school I served a church in rural south Alabama where most of the members operated large farms. Their livelihood depended on God sending rain at the proper times. To this day, these were some of the most godly, faithful people I've ever met. One of the most successful farmers told me the secret to his success. He took me behind his house and told me that his farm belonged to

God and that he had printed this verse (from the King James Version) over the door of his largest barn: "A land which the LORD thy God careth for: the eyes of the LORD thy God are always upon it, from the beginning of the year even unto the end of the year" (11:12).

Why would it take faith to believe God could take care of the Israelites in the wilderness?

How does God personally demonstrate that He cares for you?

GOD WANTS TO BE WORSHIPED (DEUT. 11:13-32)

God's love is unconditional. There's nothing we can do to earn it. But God's blessings are conditional. That means that God promises to bless us if we will obey and worship Him. He said,

> If you carefully obey my commands I am giving you today, to love the LORD your God and worship Him with all your heart and all your soul, I will provide rain for your land in the proper time, the autumn and spring rains, and you will harvest your grain, new wine, and oil (11:13-14).

When Jesus spoke with the Samaritan woman at the well, she asked Him about the proper place to worship—Gerizim or Jerusalem? Jesus responded that *where* one worships isn't as important as *how* one worships. He told her, "But an hour is coming, and is now here, when the true worshipers will worship the Father in spirit and truth. Yes, the Father wants such people to worship Him. God is spirit, and those who worship Him must worship in spirit and truth" (John 4:23-24).

God wants us to worship Him. Will you choose to worship Him?

God has given each of us the ability to make choices. He doesn't force us to love Him or obey Him. It would be sad if God made us carbon-based androids so that when He wanted to be worshiped, He only had to press a computer key in heaven and we would fall on our knees in worship. God wants our worship to be motivated by our love for Him.

All choices have consequences. If you put a child in a room with a jar of candy and tell him not to touch the jar, the child has a choice. If instead you lock the jar in a cabinet and tell the child not to touch it, the child has no choice.

That's that way it is with God. If God removed all the bad choices, we would have no freedom to choose. Instead, He loves us so much that He gives us the freedom to choose. Will you choose to worship your Creator?

Why is freedom of choice the ultimate expression of love?

What are the benefits of choosing to worship God?

BE CAREFUL HOW YOU LIVE (DEUT. 12:1–13:18)

When I was a teenager, getting ready to leave the house to drive somewhere, my mother always had the same advice for me. Without fail, she would say, "Have fun, and be careful." Of course, at the time I thought that I had to be careless to have fun! I've since learned the error of that mind-set.

Teenagers aren't the only ones who try to live careless lives. Careless living at any age can lead to destruction.

Moses was the spiritual parent of this anxious generation. As they prepared for the challenge of their lives, he told them five times in these few verses to "be careful." He said,

> Be careful to follow these statutes and ordinances in the land that Yahweh, the God of your fathers, has given you to possess all the days you live on the earth (12:1).
>
> Be careful not to offer your burnt offerings in all the sacred places you see (12:13).
>
> Be careful to obey all these things I command you, so that you and your children after you may prosper forever (12:28).
>
> Be careful not to be ensnared by their ways after they have been destroyed before you (12:30).

He summarized his "be careful" speech with a final principle: "You must be careful to do everything I command you; do not add anything to it or take anything away from it" (12:32).

This is a wonderful principle to follow regarding the entire Bible. We should be careful not to add anything to it, nor take anything away from it. This principle is repeated on the final page of your Bible when John wrote,

> I testify to everyone who hears the prophetic words of this book: If anyone adds to them, God will add to him the plagues that are written in this book. And if anyone takes away from the words of this prophetic book, God will take away his share of the tree of life and the holy city, written in this book (Rev. 22:18-19).

I knew an old preacher who liked to say, "Every command in the Bible is God's way of saying, 'Help yourself to happiness.'" When you choose to obey everything God commands you, that good choice brings more blessings.

Moses added this promise to those who choose to obey God: "You will eat there in the presence of the Lord your God and rejoice with your household in everything you do, because the Lord your God has blessed you" (Deut. 12:7).

Why do you think Moses used the phrase, "Be careful ..." when instructing the Israelites?

How do you experience God's blessings in your everyday life?

GOD CARES ABOUT WHAT YOU EAT (DEUT. 14:1-21)

The first time I remember reading the word "kosher" was on a jar of dill pickles in the grocery store. I just assumed it was a flavor. I later learned that kosher is the English pronunciation of the Hebrew word *kasher* which refers to foods that conform to the Jewish dietary laws called *kashrut*.

The two main lists of kosher foods are found in Leviticus 11 and here in Deuteronomy 14. When you compare these two lists, there are prohibitions against eating pork, shrimp, shellfish, and many types of seafood. For instance, catfish wouldn't be a kosher food because it has a skin, not scales. Other prohibited food included most insects, scavenger birds, and various other animals.

God gave the Israelites these kosher laws because He wanted them to be different from the other cultures. He said, "For you are a holy people belonging to the LORD your God" (14:21).

I love the food when I visit Israel, even though the kosher laws are still enforced. The most interesting kosher law is, "You must not boil a young goat in its mother's milk" (14:21). The Jews interpret that to mean that meat and milk should never be served together. For example, at the McDonald's restaurants in Israel, you can order a burger and fries, but you'll never find a cheeseburger on the menu. That would mix meat and milk. When we have meals in the restaurants, some are "meat meals" with no diary products. And some are "milk meals" with no meat. For instance, breakfast is a milk meal. You can find eggs, cereal, milk, cheese, and plenty of great bread, but, of course, no bacon with the eggs—or any meat!

Christians sometimes wonder if we should obey the Jewish kosher laws. It's your choice. It might make you healthier, but it won't make you holier. These rules were never intended to apply to anyone other than the Israelites.

Jesus declared all foods clean (Mark 7:19). And God gave Peter a dream in which he declared that formerly unclean animals could be eaten (Acts 10:15).

Under grace, God is more interested in how we eat, or how much we eat, rather than what we eat. In the New Testament our physical appetites are an analogy of our ability to control ourselves. If we are unable to control our eating habits, we are probably also unable to control other habits. We are not to let our appetites control us; rather we are to control them.

Why do you think God chose food preparation as a way to make the Israelites stand out from other cultures?

What does it mean for us to live "under grace" today?

» LEARNING ACTIVITY

COVENANT LIVING

Deuteronomy 14 outlines dietary and financial guidelines related to the old covenant. Why did God care about what the people ate and how they spent their money?

Ezekiel 36:26-27 describes the new covenant God would establish through Christ. "I will place My Spirit within you and cause you to follow My statutes and carefully observe My ordinances" (v. 27). How can the way we eat and spend money today reflect the honor and glory of God?

GOD DESERVES YOUR FIRST AND BEST (DEUT. 14:22-29)

Christians are familiar with giving a tithe to the Lord. But the meaning and practice of the tithe is often misunderstood. First, some Christians think the word *tithe* is a religious word. They rank it alongside the words such as "worship, serve, and pray." But the word simply means "one tenth." It's like the word "half" (50 percent) and "quarter" (25 percent). Through the years well meaning people have told me something like, "I tithe five percent of my income." You could say, "I give five percent" but it makes no sense to say, "I tithe five percent" because of the meaning of the word *tithe*.

A second misunderstanding is that when the Jews tithed, they always gave away one-tenth. But there is evidence that their tithe of grain or livestock was taken to the place of worship and they shared a meal of their tithe with the Levites. Thus they got to enjoy some of the benefits of their tithe. Moses said,

> Each year you are to set aside a tenth of all the produce grown in your fields. You are to eat a tenth of your grain, new wine, and oil, and the firstborn of your herd and flock, in the presence of Yahweh your God at the place where He chooses to have His name dwell, so that you will always learn to fear the LORD your God ... Do not neglect the Levite within your gates, since he has no portion or inheritance among you (14:22-23,27).

When God spoke through Malachi He said, "Bring the full tenth into the storehouse so that there may be food in My house" (Mal. 3:10). This fulfilled the same purpose that Moses instructed. In an agriculturally based economy, the food would be used to feed the Levites who carried out the Lord's work in the place of worship.

Some Christians insist that we are no longer obligated to tithe because it was part of the Old Testament Law, which has passed away. But I still teach and practice that giving God a tenth of our income is a great starting place to worship God through giving. Why do I believe this?

The tithe predated the Law. The first mention of tithing is found in Genesis 14:20 where Abram gives Melchizedek a tenth of all he had.

Tithing became a law under the Mosaic covenant. The only time Jesus mentioned tithing was in the context of pronouncing woes upon the Pharisees who tithed meticulously. He said, "But woe to you Pharisees! You give a tenth of mint, rue, and every kind of herb, and you bypass justice and love for God. These things you should have done without neglecting the others" (Luke 11:42).

Note that Jesus indicated that tithing is something they "should have done." But He also points out that there are other spiritual acts that are more valuable than tithing—justice and love for God.

The issue is about honoring God. When a Christian pays all his other bills and then gives God some of the leftover, that doesn't honor God.

Solomon had a good idea when he said, "Honor the Lord with your possessions and with the first produce of your entire harvest; then your barns will be completely filled, and your vats will overflow with new wine" (Prov. 3:9-10). Are you honoring God with your possessions?

For years I have taught people a simple, God-honoring stewardship plan called the 10-10-80 Plan. You give God the first tenth of your income. Then you faithfully save 10 percent of your income and you manage your expenses to be able to live on no more than 80 percent of your income. It works, and you can honor God!

What is the purpose of giving away a portion of your income?

What have you learned about God and yourself through the practice of tithing?

GOD'S PLAN IS BEST (DEUT. 15:1–18:14)

In the remaining chapters of this section, God presents an organizational plan for Israel to follow. In Deuteronomy 15, He details some fair financial practices for the Jews.

Moses said, "When the Lord your God blesses you as He has promised you, you will lend to many nations but not borrow; you will rule over many nations, but they will not rule over you" (15:6).

If you want to be financially secure, you should follow God's advice. Don't borrow unless it's absolutely necessary. When you borrow, you are a slave to the one who lends to you (Prov. 22:7). Whenever you save and invest your money, you are actually lending it.

In Deuteronomy 16, Moses outlined the three main annual festivals. Passover was celebrated to recount the amazing story of God's deliverance from bondage in Egypt. The Festival of Weeks was to celebrate the annual harvest that God had given them. The Festival of Booths was to commemorate the 40 years they lived in temporary shelters in the desert.

Although believers are no longer required to celebrate these festivals, there is an important lesson we can learn. God told them to gather with their families to celebrate and rejoice. We have holidays when we pause to give thanks to God. For example, we have holidays to celebrate the incarnation and resurrection of Jesus. Like the Jews, we should avoid all the commercial distractions of our holidays and focus on gathering with our loved ones and rejoicing together.

Why is good money management essential for a blessed life?

God loves a celebration! What choices can you make to celebrate God's goodness more often?

A CLOSER LOOK
THE MESSIAH PROPHET
(Deut. 18:17-19)

In these verses is one of the many Messianic prophecies scattered throughout the pages of the Old Testament. Moses told the Israelites that God was going to "raise up for you a prophet like me" (18:15). He recalled a time when God said, "I will raise up for them a prophet like you from among their brothers. I will put My words in his mouth, and he will tell them everything I command him. I will hold accountable whoever does not listen to My words that he speaks in My name" (18:18-19).

Jesus came as the fulfillment of this prophecy. The Jews were looking for this great "Prophet" that Moses had predicted. After Jesus fed the 5,000 with only two fish and five loaves the Bible says, "When the people saw the sign He had done, they said, 'This really is the Prophet who was to come into the world!'" (John 6:14).

As Moses predicted, Jesus claimed to be the Prophet who spoke the words that God gave Him. "For I have not spoken on My own, but the Father Himself who sent Me has given Me a command as to what I should say and what I should speak. I know that His command is eternal life. So the things that I speak, I speak just as the Father has told Me" (John 12:49-50).

What would you say to someone who asked you, "How do you know for certain that Jesus really is the promised Messiah?"

CHAPTER 5

GOD'S CHARACTER DEMONSTRATED IN RELATIONSHIPS

DEUTERONOMY 19–26

English Poet, John Donne, wrote, "No man is an island, entire of itself; every man is a piece of the continent, a part of the main." We all enjoy being alone occasionally. Periods of quiet solitude are important for emotional health. But, as nice as it may seem, we cannot simply retreat from the world permanently. We share this world with others, and we must learn how to live in relationship with them. Moses has been telling the Israelites how to live in a right relationship with God. In this section he gives them relational principles to practice among themselves and the nations that they will encounter. God's character is seen by the way He expects us to deal with others.

What is the difference between enjoying periods of solitude and isolating yourself from others?

GOD DEMANDS FAIRNESS (DEUT. 19:1–21:17)

At our church, we have a motto we often say: "Life isn't fair; but God is good." There are many things that happen in the world that disrupt our sense of "fairness." We assume that life should treat everyone equally and fairly, but that is a myth. There are others who would say that God isn't fair. That attitude reflects an understanding of both God's nature and the meaning of fairness.

When you study this section of Deuteronomy, you discover that God directs His people to treat one another with fairness and kindness.

For instance, if you had a wooden stake marking your property line, and your neighbor pulls it up and moves it, you would say, "Hey, that's not fair!" And God would agree. He said, "You must not move your neighbor's boundary marker, established at the start in the inheritance you will receive in the land the Lord your God is giving you to possess" (19:14).

How would you feel if someone falsely accused you of a wrongdoing? It would be your word against his. If you were arrested because of his accusation, you'd say, "That's not fair!" God agrees. That's why He established a principle that is still used in our American justice system. He said, "One witness cannot establish any wrongdoing or sin against a person, whatever that person has done. A fact must be established by the testimony of two or three witnesses" (19:15).

God also established a fair legal principle of equity. This principle states that crime cannot go unpunished, but the scope of the punishment should match the crime. He said, "You must not show pity: life for life, eye for eye, tooth for tooth, hand for hand, and foot for foot" (19:21).

That might sound harsh, but at the time, it represented a quantum leap in fairness. Before this principle, if a man killed another man, the dead man's family would not only kill the killer, they would also kill the family of the killer. If a man gouged out another man's eye in a fight, the one-eyed man would try to gouge out both eyes of his attacker. Get the idea?

» LEARNING ACTIVITY

GRACE

Deuteronomy 19–21 describes God's rules to govern the fairness between individuals. Fairness is a trait of God's nature. As His children, we are to reflect that nature to others. In the New Testament, God displays fairness to a new level as He extends grace toward us. Grace is described as the undeserved favor of God and His saving activity manifested in the gift of Jesus who took our place and died for our sin.

Using this acrostic, how would you define God's grace?

G

R

A

C

E

Jesus came to complete the Old Testament law. He introduced something much better than fairness—He showed us grace. Referring to this passage in Deuteronomy He said, "You have heard that it was said, An eye for an eye and a tooth for a tooth. But I tell you, don't resist an evildoer. On the contrary, if anyone slaps you on your right cheek, turn the other to him also" (Matt. 5:38-39).

As followers of Jesus Christ, we don't live by the rule of fairness. We live under grace.

A SON CANNOT DISHONOR HIS FATHER (DEUT. 21:18-21)

God gave these instructions about punishing a rebellious son:

> If a man has a stubborn and rebellious son who does not obey his father or mother and doesn't listen to them even after they discipline him, his father and mother must take hold of him and bring him to the elders of his city, to the gate of his hometown. They will say to the elders of his city, 'This son of ours is stubborn and rebellious; he doesn't obey us. He's a glutton and a drunkard.' Then all the men of his city will stone him to death. You must purge the evil from you, and all Israel will hear and be afraid (21:18-21).

There have probably been more than a few frustrated parents of modern teenagers who have wanted to apply this verse! But does this seem to reflect the same fairness of the other laws? The behavior of a son was a direct reflection on the honor of his father. God was teaching the Israelites that, as holy people, their bad behavior was a poor reflection on God's character.

Understanding this law will help you better appreciate grace. In Luke 15 Jesus told a story about a rebellious son who demanded his inheritance and left home to spend it on wild living. We call him the Prodigal Son because he spent his inheritance lavishly and recklessly on riotous living. He ended up feeding pigs in a very non-kosher environment.

When he came to his senses, he returned to his father with the plan of asking to become a servant instead of a son. This son had dishonored his father. His wicked behavior was a poor reflection on his father's character.

I'm certain that when Jesus was telling this story, all the listeners were thinking about this passage in Deuteronomy. They were Jews who knew what God's Word prescribed for rebellious sons. They expected the story to end with a public stoning—after all, that would have been the "fair" thing to do.

But Jesus taught that grace trumps fairness. In this story, the father came running to meet his rebellious son. He hugged him and lavished him with clothes and food.

Why does a Christian's bad behavior reflect poorly on God?

How does it make you feel to know you are God's representative on earth?

A CLOSER LOOK

ANYONE HUNG ON A TREE IS CURSED (Deut. 21:22-23)

In this section God instructs the Jews to show respect even for those who are executed. He said, "If anyone is found guilty of an offense deserving the death penalty and is executed, and you hang his body on a tree, you are not to leave his corpse on the tree overnight but are to bury him that day, for anyone hung on a tree is under God's curse" (21:22-23a).

The first time we read the word "curse" is in Genesis 3. Adam and Eve had disobeyed God, and the result of their sin was a curse upon the earth.

In his wonderful Christmas song, "Joy to the World," Isaac Watts wrote about this curse. "No more let sins and sorrows grow, nor thorns infest the ground; He comes to make His blessings flow, Far as the curse is found."

The curse of sin is worldwide. Thorns grow on every continent except Antarctica. In Genesis 3 God pronounced that part of the curse of sin was that thorns and thistles would grow and infest the ground. Thorns represent the broken relationship between God and man.

When Abraham was getting ready to sacrifice Isaac, there was a ram caught in—guess what? Thorns. The ram that became a substitute for Isaac was literally wearing a crown of thorns. And then 2,000 years after Abraham took Isaac as a sacrifice on Mt. Moriah, Jesus was walking up another part of Mt. Moriah as our sacrifice. And He was wearing a crown of thorns. And today, we rejoice that in wearing that crown and dying on that cross takes away the curse of sin.

Paul summarized it this way, "Christ has redeemed us from the curse of the law by becoming a curse for us, because it is written: Everyone who is hung on a tree is cursed" (Gal. 3:13).

In what way is sin a curse?

How did Jesus break the curse of sin?

GOD EXPECTS RESPECT FOR ANIMALS (DEUT. 22:1-4)

In addition to having relationships with people, we live in a world where we have relationships with God's creatures called animals. God directs His people to show respect to animals. He told them:

> If you see your brother's ox or sheep straying, you must not ignore it; make sure you return it to your brother. If your brother does not live near you or you don't know him, you are to bring the animal to your home to remain with you until your brother comes looking for it; then you can return it to him. Do the same for his donkey, his garment, or anything your brother has lost and you have found. You must not ignore it. If you see your brother's donkey or ox fallen down on the road, you must not ignore it; you must help him lift it up (22:1-4).

How a person treats animals is often a reflection about how he or she treats people. A person who is kind to animals will usually be kind to people. But a person who treats animals with cruelty should be watched carefully; he or she may treat people the same way.

The writer of Proverbs expressed it this way: "A righteous man cares about his animal's health, but even the merciful acts of the wicked are cruel" (Prov. 12:10).

When we show kindness to animals, we are imitating God's heart because God cares for the animals. Psalm 147:9 says that God spreads His wings over all His creation and feeds the cattle and the young raven when they call. He owns "every animal" and "the cattle on a thousand hills" (Ps. 50:10). In His final word to Jonah, God said that He cared for all the inhabits of Nineveh as well as their animals.

What does God's care for animals teach you about His character?

GOD REQUIRES SEXUAL PURITY (DEUT. 22:5-23:18)

We live in a sex-saturated society. It's hard to live a G-rated life in an X-rated culture. We think that this is a modern problem, but there have always been sexual sins. Many of the pagan fertility religions utilized sex as part of their worship ritual. That's why God issued this prohibition; "No Israelite woman is to be a cult prostitute, and no Israelite man is to be a cult prostitute. Do not bring a female prostitute's wages or a male prostitute's earnings into the house of the Lord your God to fulfill any vow, because both are detestable to the Lord your God" (23:17-18).

During these days when gay-rights activists are demanding that we normalize sin, we sometimes lose sight of the fact that God despises adultery as much as homosexual activity. He said, "If a man is discovered having sexual relations with another man's wife, both the man who had sex with the woman and the woman must die. You must purge the evil from Israel" (22:22).

Christians must have a healthy understanding about what God's Word says about sexual behavior. God created sex for two purposes. First, it is to express the deepest physical intimacy between a husband and wife in marriage. Second, it is to propagate the human race.

After God created Eve and gave her to Adam He explained marriage to them. He said, "This is why a man leaves his father and mother and bonds with his wife, and they become one flesh. Both the man and his wife were naked, yet felt no shame" (Gen. 2:24-25).

It's simple to identify what sexual purity is—it's sex between a man and woman in the marriage relationship. Any sexual behavior outside that is sexual sin.

Of course, some men in the Old Testament had multiple wives. In Genesis 4, Lamech was the first man to have two wives, but God didn't tell him to take two wives. God's only provision for multiple wives was in the case of Levirate marriage (discussed later in this chapter). Solomon had a thousand wives, but the Bible says his wives turned his heart from God. But from the beginning, God's plan was one man and one woman. God gave Adam only one wife. Leaders in the church are to be husbands of one wife, and in Ephesians 5:25 Paul wrote, "Husbands, love your wives, just as Christ loved the church."

Why is our sexuality precious to God? Why does He care so much about our sexuality?

How can you protect yourself from sexual temptation?

» LEARNING ACTIVITY

AN X-RATED CULTURE

God calls us, His children, to live in sexual purity. Our culture, however, makes that very difficult. For each of the topics listed, note recent examples that challenge us in the area of sexual purity.

Entertainers
Television
Movies
Music
Clothing
Advertising

For this last one, they say "sex sells." What are some common items (such as toothpaste) that you have seen sold with sexually provocative advertising?

God demands sexual purity today. If you're married, stay true to your mate. If you're single, abstain from sex until God gives you a mate. Of course, the Bible is full of characters who messed up sexually. Lot committed incest. Abraham had sex with his wife's handmaid. Rahab was a prostitute. Samson was a one-man sexual tornado. David committed adultery with Bathsheba. These were real people like us who struggled with sexual temptation. God forgave them, like He can forgive us. But each of them suffered the consequences of ignoring God's sexual boundaries.

GOD CHERISHES MARRIAGE (DEUT. 24:1-5)

The subject of divorce is one of the most hotly debated topics among Christians. There is hardly a church or a family that hasn't had to deal with it. We're so obsessed debating the theological significance of divorce that we sometimes overlook the pain and heartache that is created in divorce.

In Matthew 19 a Pharisee was questioning Jesus about divorce. "'Why then,' they asked Him, 'did Moses command us to give divorce papers and to send her away?'" (Matt. 19:7).

We'll examine Jesus' reply later. However, let's take the time to discover what Moses said about divorce. His directions in Deuteronomy 24 were:

> If a man marries a woman, but she becomes displeasing to him because he finds something improper about her, he may write her a divorce certificate, hand it to her, and send her away from his house. If after leaving his house she goes and becomes another man's wife, and the second man hates her, writes her a divorce certificate, hands it to her, and sends her away from his house or if he dies, the first husband who sent her away may not marry her again after she has been defiled, because that would be detestable to the LORD. You must not bring guilt on the land the LORD your God is giving you as an inheritance (24:1-4).

The context of Moses' instructions addressed the question of what happens if the divorced woman is divorced or widowed by her second husband. Moses allowed divorce if the husband found "something improper" about his wife. The literal translation is "indecency." This could range from sexual sin, to being infertile, or having a nagging personality. The rabbis were deeply divided on how to define it.

Confusion still reigns today about "grounds" for divorce. Notice the reply of Jesus when asked about Moses' divorce decree. "He told them, 'Moses permitted you to divorce your wives because of the hardness of your hearts. But it was not like that from the beginning. And I tell you, whoever divorces his wife, except for sexual immorality, and marries another, commits adultery'" (Matt. 19:8-9).

It's neither popular, nor politically correct, but there are no biblical grounds for divorce. In the cases of adultery and abuse, there may be reasons for divorce, but God's perfect plan has always been one man and one woman until death separates them. Divorce represents a violation of a vow before God. I've known many believers who have lived through the sins of divorce and remarriage by admitting their sin to God and making a commitment to be faithful to their current mate.

What is your understanding of what the Bible teaches about divorce?

How does God demonstrate forgiveness and grace, despite a divorce?

GOD VALUES FAMILIES (DEUT. 24:6–25:19)

As God's people were poised to enter Israel, they needed every able-bodied person they could muster. The greatest blessings God gave to the Israelites were children—especially sons. If a woman lost her husband and she had no children, then she was destitute with no standing within the community. For this reason, God instructed the dead man's brother to take his widow as his own wife. If she could bear children from her husband's brother, they were to maintain the name of her original husband. This practice was called Levirate Marriage. It comes from the Latin word *levir,* meaning "husband's brother."

If there was no living brother, this law extended to other family members as well. In the beautiful story of Ruth, she was not free to marry Boaz because there was a closer relative to Elimelech, Naomi's deceased husband. Only after the closer relative gave up his rights to redeem Naomi's land, was Boaz free to marry Ruth.

This rather strange law is simply a testimony of how God values families. The Bible says, "Sons are indeed a heritage from the LORD, children, a reward. Like arrows in the hand of a warrior are the sons born in one's youth. Happy is the man who has filled his quiver with them" (Ps. 127:3-5a).

What does the value God places on families tell you about His nature?

How do you demonstrate the priority of family?

GOD HONORS THOSE WHO HONOR HIM (DEUT. 26:1-19)

It has been my joy to participate in a ceremony of the renewal of the marriage vows for dozens of couples. It usually happens on a significant anniversary. A renew of commitment is a way to say, "I still love you. I will still be faithful to you."

God gave Generation 2.0 a chance to renew their commitment to His covenant. Moses officiated at this reaffirmation:

> Today you have affirmed that the Lord is your God and that you will walk in His ways, keep His statutes, commands, and ordinances, and obey Him. And today the Lord has affirmed that you are His special people as He promised you, that you are to keep all His commands, that He will elevate you to praise, fame, and glory above all the nations He has made, and that you will be a holy people to the Lord your God as He promised (26:17-19).

In what areas do you need to consider renewing your commitment to God? (Examples: Bible reading, fellowship with other Christians, your marriage, etc.)

How would that decision change the way you relate to others?

CHAPTER 6

GOD'S PROMISES DECLARED

DEUTERONOMY 27–28

When I was a child, one of my favorite television shows was the *Twilight Zone,* which ran from 1959 to 1964. One of the most popular episodes was called, "A Most Unusual Camera." A husband-and-wife team robbed a curio shop and one of the things they stole was a camera. But this camera produced pictures from about five minutes in the future. Realizing a potential to cash in on this unusual camera, they went to the racetrack and took a picture of the betting board before the race began. They made thousands of dollars by betting on the winning horses. But there is no honor among thieves and another crook showed up. In the process of arguing over the camera, they fell out of the upstairs window, but when the wife took their picture, she was also seen lying on the ground—sure enough a crooked waiter from the hotel arrived and pushed her out.

People are fascinated with the future. But you don't need a magic camera or a horoscope to learn about the future. The Bible gives us fully developed pictures of what's going to happen in the future. And in this passage, God gives us a snapshot of what life in the promised land would be like for the Israelites.

Prophecy is history written in reverse. The Bible is full of prophetic promises. This section of Deuteronomy contains some of the most remarkable prophecies in the entire Word of God.

INSCRIBE GOD'S LAWS IN STONE (DEUT. 27:1-10)

God instructed the Israelites to make a lasting record of His law. Much of the Jewish Law and history has been passed down from generation to generation through oral recounting. But God has always wanted a written record as well.

"Moses and the elders of Israel commanded the people, 'Keep every command I am giving you today. At the time you cross the Jordan into the land the Lord your God is giving you, you must set up large stones and cover them with plaster. Write all the words of this law on the stones after you cross to enter the land the Lord your God is giving you, a land flowing with milk and honey, as Yahweh, the God of your fathers, has promised you'" (27:1-3).

The first thing God instructed them to do when they entered the land was to set up a monument that would preserve a written record of His law. Today, in the Bible, we have a precious written record of God's redemptive story. But we also have something better than Moses had. We have God's law written on our hearts. God predicted through the prophet Jeremiah,

> I will put My teaching within them and write it on their hearts. I will be their God, and they will be My people. No longer will one teach his neighbor or his brother, saying, 'Know the LORD,' for they will all know Me, from the least to the greatest of them"—this is the LORD's declaration. "For I will forgive their wrongdoing and never again remember their sin (Jer. 31:33-34).

» LEARNING ACTIVITY

SCRIPTURE MEMORIZATION

In Deuteronomy 27:1-10, the people were instructed to write God's laws on stones—a permanent reminder of His instructions. Today, we have the Scriptures in print and digital forms that we can read whenever we want. Scripture memorization is one way to keep portions of God's Word with us everywhere. The following verses all address the importance of putting God's Word into your heart. Spend several minutes each day this week committing the verse to memory.

Deuteronomy 6:6-7
Deuteronomy 30:14
Psalm 119:11
Jeremiah 15:16
John 17:17
Colossians 3:16

Choose one verse from the above list you will memorize this week:

At the same place where they built a monument to the Law, God also instructed them to construct an altar for worship. He said, "Build an altar of stones there to the LORD your God—you must not use any iron tool on them. Use uncut stones to build the altar of the LORD your God and offer burnt offerings to the LORD your God on it. There you are to sacrifice fellowship offerings, eat, and rejoice in the presence of the LORD your God" (Deut. 27:5-7).

The monument would be a record of the words and the altar would be a place a prayer. That is a good reminder to us that God's Word and prayer must always be together.

How do you demonstrate reverence for God's Word?

A CLOSER LOOK

Jesus Our Altar

The altar God instructed the Israelites to make in Deuteronomy 27 was to be made of uncut stones. This is a picture of Jesus, who is our Altar. He is the Stone that was not cut with human hands. In Daniel's interpretation of Nebuchadnezzar's dream of the future kingdoms, he identified this Stone as one that would fill the earth.

The Bible says, "As you were watching, a stone broke off without a hand touching it, struck the statue on its feet of iron and fired clay, and crushed them. Then the iron, the fired clay, the bronze, the silver, and the gold were shattered and became like chaff from the summer threshing floors. The wind carried them away, and not a trace of them could be found. But the stone that struck the statue became a great mountain and filled the whole earth" (Dan. 2:34-35).

Jesus was born of a virgin, and yet became the Rock of our salvation. We no longer have a need for man-made altars because He is our Rock of Ages, cut only by God.

SHOUT GOD'S WORD FROM THE MOUNTAIN TOPS (DEUT. 27:11-26)

Moses instructed the Israelites: "When you have crossed the Jordan, these tribes will stand on Mount Gerizim to bless the people: Simeon, Levi, Judah, Issachar, Joseph, and Benjamin. And these tribes will stand on Mount Ebal to deliver the curse: Reuben, Gad, Asher, Zebulun, Dan, and Naphtali" (27:12-13).

The six tribes appointed to announce the blessing were all the children of the free wives of Jacob. The Levites formed a special group to pronounce the blessings and curses. In response to each pronouncement the congregation responded by shouting, "Amen!"

There are two Hebrew words that are used by believers around the world: "hallelujah" and "amen." The Hebrew word *amen* appears 23 times in the Old Testament, and over half of those occurrences are in these verses. The word means, "so be it." We use "amen" to conclude our prayers, and when we agree with a statement that we have heard. In years past, churches used to have an "amen corner" where members of the congregation would sit and verbally affirm what the pastor was preaching. It often located near the "mourners bench" where sinners confessing their faults would weep over their sin.

Saying, "amen" to a preacher seems to be a dying art form. It's sad that most Americans now identify "amen corner" with three golf holes at Augusta National Golf Club rather than a place where biblical truth was affirmed.

Below: Standing on Mount Gerizim looking across at Mount Ebal. The city of Nablus (biblical Shechem) can be seen in the valley below.

ILLUSTRATOR PHOTO/ BOB SCHATZ (9/24/11)

I heard the late Dr. Adrian Rogers say once that we won't experience a revival in our churches until we have a visit from "Mr. Amen" and "Mr. Wet Eyes" again.

Why do we sometimes lose enthusiasm in our faith?

What can you do to restore your enthusiasm and excitement for your faith?

OBEY GOD AND YOU'LL BE BLESSED (DEUT. 28:1-14)

I was driving through New Mexico a few years ago and was surprised to find a city on the map named Truth or Consequences. I wondered how they got that name, so I made a detour to visit the strangely named town. I discovered that Truth or Consequences is a beautiful resort city. It was formerly named Hot Springs, New Mexico. Back in the 1940's there was a popular NBC radio program named *Truth or Consequences*. In 1950, Ralph Edwards, the host of the show announced that he would air the program from the first town in America that would rename itself after the show. Hot Springs won the honor. Until his death, Ralph Edwards continued to visit the city annually for a city celebration.

We're familiar with the term "truth or consequences." But in the Bible, it is more appropriate to say that God's Word gives truth *and* consequences. God told the Israelites that if they obeyed His truth, there would be positive consequences. But if they disobeyed His law, there would be negative consequences.

In the first verses of chapter 28 God gave them a preview of what their nation would become if they obeyed Him. Some commentators have observed that Deuteronomy 28 is the pre-written history of the nation of Israel.

Moses said, "Now if you faithfully obey the LORD your God and are careful to follow all His commands I am giving you today, the LORD your God will put you far above all the nations of the earth. All these blessings will come and overtake you, because you obey the LORD your God" (28:1-2).

We know from reading the Books of Joshua, Judges, Kings, and Chronicles what actually transpired over the next few generations. The Israelites obeyed God, and He blessed them just as He promised. There was a period in their history when God truly put them far above all the nations of the earth.

Moses promised, "The LORD will establish you as His holy people, as He swore to you, if you obey the commands of the LORD your God and walk in His ways. Then all the peoples of the earth will see that you are called by Yahweh's name, and they will stand in awe of you" (28:9-10).

From the hindsight of history, we see this prophecy fulfilled during the reigns of King David and King Solomon. Once David consolidated the different tribes, he established a stable kingdom. Under Solomon's leadership, Israel reached the pinnacle of wealth and prominence among the nations.

At the apex of Solomon's reign, Queen Sheba from the south visited Solomon. She came to observe if what she had heard about the wealth and wisdom of Solomon was true.

> When the queen of Sheba observed all of Solomon's wisdom, the palace he had built, the food at his table, his servants' residence, his attendants' service and their attire, his cupbearers, and the burnt offerings he offered at the Lord's temple, it took her breath away.
>
> She said to the king, "The report I heard in my own country about your words and about your wisdom is true. But I didn't believe the reports until I came and saw with my own eyes. Indeed, I was not even told half" (1 Kings 10:4-7).

And yet, tragically, the Bible says that when Solomon was old, his wives turned his heart from God. And the kingdom that had been so blessed by obeying God began a long, slow cycle into disobedience and punishment. But Moses also predicted the consequences of disobedience.

How do you recognize God's blessings in your life?

When was a time you experienced a great blessing from God as a result of your obedience?

CONSEQUENCES COME WHEN YOU IGNORE GOD'S LAWS (DEUT. 28:15-35)

The Bible reveals the truth of God's Word and the consequences of both obedience and rebellion. Moses clearly warned the people about the negative consequences of rebellion. "But if you do not obey the LORD your God by carefully following all His commands and statutes I am giving you today, all these curses will come and overtake you" (28:15).

God never intended for His laws to become a substitute for the blessing of each individual having a personal relationship with Him. He had established a covenant relationship with the Israelites, and He took their disobedience as a personal insult. He said, "The LORD will send against you curses, confusion, and rebuke in everything you do until you are destroyed and quickly perish, because of the wickedness of your actions in abandoning Me" (28:20). Their real sin was not breaking rules. Their mistake was abandoning the God who had delivered them.

God never intended for His laws to become a substitute for the blessing of each individual having a personal relationship with Him.

The descriptions of the potential curses read like the previews to a horror movie—and it would be R-rated. These horrible consequences include pestilence, disease, drought, corpses devoured by animals, blindness, rape, robbery, human trafficking, hunger, and cannibalism.

Why does God take disobedience so personally?

Where do you see the consequences of wickedness in our culture today?

A PROPHECY OF FUTURE EXILE (DEUT. 28:36-57)

In one of the clearest prophetic passages, Moses made a chilling prediction that Israel would be invaded and removed from their land. That was the next chapter in Israel's history after the wealth and prominence under Solomon. He said, "The LORD will bring you and your king that you have appointed to a nation neither you nor your fathers have known, and there you will worship other gods, of wood and stone. You will become an object of horror, scorn, and ridicule among all the peoples where the LORD will drive you" (28:36-37).

This sad prediction was fulfilled first when the Northern Kingdom of Israel fell to the Assyrians in 722 B.C. It was again fulfilled when the Babylonians invaded Judah in 586 B.C.

Moses continued to predict another horrible invasion that occurred when the Roman army, whose emblem was an eagle, laid siege to Jerusalem and utterly destroyed the city and the Holy Temple. He wrote,

> The LORD will bring a nation from far away, from the ends of the earth, to swoop down on you like an eagle, a nation whose language you don't understand, a ruthless nation, showing no respect for the old and not sparing the young ... They will besiege you within all your gates until your high and fortified walls, that you trust in, come down throughout your land. They will besiege you within all your gates throughout the land the LORD your God has given you (28:49-50,52).

Jesus made the same prediction when He stood and wept over Jerusalem the week before His crucifixion. His descriptions of the horrors of this event concur with the words of Moses.

> As He approached and saw the city, He wept over it, saying, "If you knew this day what would bring peace—but now it is hidden from your eyes. For the days will come on you when your enemies will build an embankment against you, surround you, and hem you in on every side. They will crush you and your children within you to the ground, and they will not leave one stone on another in you, because you did not recognize the time of your visitation" (Luke 19:41-44).

The Jewish historian, Josephus, wrote an account of the siege of Jerusalem in A.D. 70. His horrific descriptions of the misery of the Israelites under attack sound hauntingly similar to the warnings of Moses.

God goes to the trouble to warn us against bad behavior. What do His warnings reveal about His nature and His love for us?

THE HEARTACHE OF REJECTING GOD (DEUT. 28:58-68)

Again from the hindsight of history, we recognize that Deuteronomy 28 is a prophecy of Israel's future destiny. They were a nation singularly blessed by Yahweh, and attained global prominence and wealth. And yet they became proud and arrogant because of their perceived "favored nation" status. The result was the sad revolving cycle of blessing, sin, punishment, repentance, and blessing again. Then the spiritual cycle repeated itself.

Along with other Bible expositors, I see an amazing prophecy in this chapter of the diaspora of the Jews. Moses predicted:

> You will be deported from the land you are entering to possess. Then the LORD will scatter you among all peoples from one end of the earth to the other ... You will find no peace among those nations, and there will be no resting place for the sole of your foot. There the LORD will give you a trembling heart, failing eyes, and a despondent spirit (28:63b-65).

After the destruction of Jerusalem in A.D. 70, the Jewish people we scattered (diaspora) to all the nations of the earth. They have never really felt at home in any of their nations. Yet throughout the generations, they have maintained their own culture.

If you've ever seen *The Fiddler on the Roof,* you understand why the songs are sung in a minor key, and there is a note of sadness, even in their times of joy.

But Paul reminded us in Romans 11 that God has not rejected His people. In my two-dozen trips to Israel, I have seen the fulfillment of the prophecy that God is re-gathering His people. First there has been a political rebuilding of Israel, and next will come a spiritual rebuilding. The time is coming when they will recognize Jesus as their Messiah. As Zechariah prophesied, "Then I will pour out a spirit of grace and prayer on the house of David and the residents of Jerusalem, and they will look at Me whom they pierced. They will mourn for Him as one mourns for an only child and weep bitterly for Him as one weeps for a firstborn" (Zech. 12:10).

What is the difference between being temporarily punished by God and being rejected by Him forever?

A CLOSER LOOK

America the Blessed

Whenever I study the history of Israel, I think about our own nation. God has blessed America like few nations. But if we become proud and believe we have "favored nation" status with God, we are making a grave mistake. If we ignore and forsake the God who has blessed us, we will face desperate consequences as well.

As President Abraham Lincoln said as he called the nation to a day of prayer and fasting in 1863,

> "We have been the recipients of the choicest bounties of Heaven; we have been preserved these many years in peace and prosperity; we have grown in numbers, wealth, and power, as no other nation has ever grown. But we have forgotten God. We have forgotten the gracious hand which preserved us in peace and multiplied and enriched and strengthened us, and we have vainly imagined, in the deceitfulness of our hearts, that all these blessings were produced by some superior wisdom and virtue of our own. Intoxicated with unbroken success, we have become too self-sufficient to feel the necessity of redeeming and preserving grace, too proud to pray to the God that made us!"

 CHAPTER 7

GOD'S COVENANT RENEWED

DEUTERONOMY 29–30

This section of Deuteronomy has been called "The Palestinian Covenant" because it deals with the land of Palestine. The current conditions in the Middle East make this title confusing. The Palestinians claim their right to the property currently occupied by Israel. God's covenant was with the Israelites and the land He had promised to them. So, it's less confusing to call this the "covenant for the land."

A COVENANT ABOUT THE PROMISED LAND (DEUT. 29:1-9)

In modern times we enter into many different business relationships by the use of a contract. A contract spells out the structure of the business relationship and what is expected of each party. For instance, when you purchase a home, you sign a contract. The seller agrees to fully surrender the property to you, and you agree to pay the agreed-upon price for the property. Unless you can pay cash, there is another party involved—a lending agency. Contracts clearly spell out the consequences of what happens if the contract is broken.

The Lord never established a contract with Israel or the church. He created a covenant with them. A covenant is a more informal agreement between two or more parties determining a specific action. Covenants involve trust. When you sign a covenant with your neighborhood association not to park an RV on the street, your neighbors trust you.

When you make an appointment to see your physician, you are making a covenant that you'll show up at the appointed time. If you fail to keep the appointment, chances are the doctor isn't going to come looking for you. He'll just go to the next patient. The only consequences of breaking this informal covenant is that you might have a harder time getting an appointment the next time you try or have to pay for an appointment you didn't keep.

When God establishes a covenant, it involves both trust and love. The Bible indicates that His covenants are more like a parent to a child rather than a physician to his patients. If your child fails to show up to a scheduled meal, you are going to seek to find that child, because you care for that son or daughter. God's covenant is described by the prophet Isaiah, "Can a woman forget her nursing child, or lack compassion for the child of her womb? Even if these forget, yet I will not forget you. Look, I have inscribed you on the palms of My hands; your walls are continually before Me" (Isa. 49:15-16).

The covenant in Deuteronomy 29 does not replace the one God made with the Israelites at Horeb (Mt. Sinai); it reinforces the one made 40 years earlier.

> These are the words of the covenant the LORD commanded Moses to make with the Israelites in the land of Moab, *in addition to* the covenant He had made with them at Horeb" (Deut. 29:1, emphasis added).

The covenant at Horeb involved the giving of the law. This additional covenant relates to the land.

This generation of Israelites would have been children and teenagers when they witnessed the first covenant. Except for Moses, Joshua, and Caleb, the oldest people in the nation would have been about 60 years old. Even as they wandered in the wilderness for 40 years, God miraculously took care of them. Can you imagine wearing the same pair of shoes for 40 years? What would it be like to wear a coat that still seemed new after you had worn it for 40 years?

And yet, in spite of these miracles, the people were still afflicted with spiritual dullness. Moses observed, "Yet to this day the LORD has not given you a mind to understand, eyes to see, or ears to hear" (29:4).

It is not for lack of evidence that people are unbelievers.

A great many people in our culture today say that if they could just see God perform a mighty miracle, then they would believe. I call these misguided people "miracle mongers." These children of Israel saw miracles for 40 years, and they were still blind to the truth. It is not for lack of evidence that people are unbelievers. Faith may produce miracles, but miracles seldom produce faith. A faith that demands a miracle isn't faith at all.

What does God's covenant to the Israelites teach you about His love?

Which of God's promises in the Bible mean the most to you and why?

Left: The plains of Moab.

ILLUSTRATOR PHOTO/ BRENT BRUCE (60/8081)

» LEARNING ACTIVITY

MY CONTRACTS

For which of the following things have you entered into a contract:
__ house __ car __ credit card __ loan __ other

What is your part of keeping each contract?

What happens if you do not keep your part of the contract?

What is the obligation of the other party in your contact?

THE COVENANT IS FOR EVERYONE (DEUT. 29:10-15)

When we imagine this enormous horde of humanity camped in the desert, we often think that all of them were descendants of Abraham, Isaac, and Jacob. However, along the way through the desert, the Israelites had enlisted non-Jews to be a part of their nation.

Moses identified the groups who were participants in this new covenant, "All of you are standing today before the LORD your God—your leaders, tribes, elders, officials, all the men of Israel, your children, your wives, and the foreigners in your camps who cut your wood and draw your water—so that you may enter into the covenant of the LORD your God, which He is making with you today" (29:10-12).

It's important to notice that God included the foreigners who worked in the camp of the Israelites. God chose the nation of Israel to be a special nation. But His divine purpose was that the Jews would take the truth of God to their Gentile neighbors. He repeated this inclusion with this promise, "I am making this covenant and this oath not only with you, but also with those who are standing here with us today in the presence of the LORD our God and with those who are not here today" (29:14-15). God included "those who are not here today." With that statement, God embraced future generations of Israelites in His covenant.

God still has a future covenant to be fulfilled with the Israelites when they recognize Jesus as their Messiah. Paul indicated that God isn't finished with the Jewish people. He wrote, "A partial hardening has come to Israel until the full number of the Gentiles has come in. And in this way all Israel will be saved, as it is written: The Liberator will come from Zion; He will turn away godlessness from Jacob. And this will be My covenant with them when I take away their sins" (Rom. 11:25-27).

How willing are you to share the hope of God's promise with others? What tempts you to keep it to yourself?

DON'T BE DECEIVED; GOD WILL NOT BE MOCKED (DEUT. 29:16-29)

Most of us are familiar with these words from Galatians, "Don't be deceived: God is not mocked. For whatever a man sows he will also reap" (Gal. 6:7).

Bad seeds lead to bad fruit. Bad thoughts lead to evil behavior. There's a similar warning in Hebrews 12:15, "Make sure that no one falls short of the grace of God and that no root of bitterness springs up, causing trouble and by it, defiling many."

The best way to understand this New Testament admonition is by studying it in the context of Deuteronomy 29. God employed strong language to warn the people about what would happen if anyone broke His covenant. "Be sure there is no root among you bearing poisonous and bitter fruit. When someone hears the words of this oath, he may consider himself exempt, thinking,

'I will have peace even though I follow my own stubborn heart'" (29:18b-19a).

The bad root is what gives birth to the bitter fruit. What is this root? It's the self-deception that we can sin with impunity. Perhaps it's part of our fallen human nature to want to test the limits. Studies have shown that when a sign saying, "Wet Paint" is placed on a park bench, the majority of people will touch it to be sure. Maybe we think that God's laws apply to everyone else, but not to us. This is a dangerous form of self-deception.

God warned the people that the tragic consequence of abandoning His covenant would be that the land itself would become desolate and barren.

> Future generations of your children who follow you and the foreigner who comes from a distant country will see the plagues of the land and the sicknesses the LORD has inflicted on it. All its soil will be a burning waste of sulfur and salt ... All the nations will ask, "Why has the LORD done this to this land?" (29:22-24a).

This is another prophecy that was fulfilled because the nation of Israel rejected God's covenant. God said that in the future, foreigners would visit the land and wonder about its desolation. In 1867, Mark Twain visited the land of Palestine and he described it as a desolate country. He wrote of "a desolate country whose soil is rich enough, but is given over wholly to weeds ... hardly a tree or shrub anywhere. Even the olive tree and cactus, those fast friends of a worthless soil, had almost deserted the country."[1]

Today, God has restored the nation of Israel. I can report firsthand that the land is no longer desolate. It is one of the most fertile countries on earth. As the Bible predicted, "the desert will rejoice and blossom like a rose" (Isa. 35:1). They are filling "the whole world with fruit" (Isa. 27:6). They export fruit to every continent.

God's ways often remain a mystery to us. That's the way He planned it. If we could understand everything about God, then we would be like God. He moves in ways that we don't understand. Moses reminded this generation, "The hidden things belong to the LORD our God, but the revealed things belong to us and our children forever, so that we may follow all the words of this law" (Deut. 29:29).

How do we deceive ourselves about the consequences of sin?

What would happen if sin had no consequence?

RETURN TO THE LORD BY OBEYING HIM (DEUT. 30:1-10)

My mother made dresses for my sister. She would go to a fabric store and buy the fabric and a pattern. The pattern was a paper template she laid on the fabric to know where to cut and where to sew. I was always fascinated that she could make a dress. But she always said that it was easy because she just followed the pattern.

In the Bible, we find a clear pattern of how God relates to His people. He loves them and calls them to Himself. He gives them directions on how to live in a relationship with Him. If they follow His directions, they are blessed. But if they rebel against Him, He sends judgment. But God doesn't reject them. He calls them back to Himself, and when the people confess and repent of their sin, He forgives them and renews His relationship with Him. He still follows that pattern today.

That pattern can be seen clearly in the first part of Deuteronomy 30. Once the people return to God from their disobedience, Moses promised:

> Then He will restore your fortunes, have compassion on you, and gather you again from all the peoples where the LORD your God has scattered you. Even if your exiles are at the ends of the earth, He will gather you and bring you back from there. The LORD your God will bring you into the land your fathers possessed, and you will take possession of it. He will cause you to prosper and multiply you more than He did your fathers. The LORD your God will circumcise your heart and the hearts of your descendants, and you will love Him with all your heart and all your soul so that you will live (30:3-6).

Bible students have often wondered why God would choose circumcision as the mark of His covenant with Abraham. Moses indicates that physical circumcision was simply an object lesson to teach a deeper truth. The removal of a piece of skin was a picture of removing anything in our hearts that would restrict our love for God. He wrote about how God will circumcise the hearts of the people so they will love Him with no reservation.

The apostle Paul reaffirmed this truth in his Letter to the Romans: "For a person is not a Jew who is one outwardly, and true circumcision is not something visible in the flesh. On the contrary, a person is a Jew who is one inwardly, and circumcision is of the heart—by the Spirit, not the letter" (Rom. 2:28-29).

How do you know that God's capacity to forgive His children is endless?

How does the experience of grace help our faith?

CHOOSE LIFE! (DEUT. 30:11-20)

Life is full of choices. As technology increases, so does our number of choices. When I was a child the only television choices we had were ABC, CBS, or NBC. Now the channel choices number in the hundreds. At the local drugstore we could choose only chocolate, vanilla, or strawberry. Today there are an infinite number of flavors from which we may choose.

I once read a humorous story about a college professor who was sitting in a boring faculty meeting. Suddenly an angel appeared to him and said, "I will grant you one of three choices—infinite wisdom, infinite wealth, or infinite health." The professor thought for a moment and said, "Wisdom." "So be it." The angel said, and then disappeared.

In a few minutes the dean of the department called on the professor to share any words of wisdom he might have. The professor said, "I should have taken the money."

There are some decisions we regret, and some decisions are easy. They are what we call "no-brainers." If your 6-year-old son asks you if he can jump off the roof using a parachute he made with bed sheets, easy decision. If you get an email from someone in Nigeria claiming to be a desperate widow who is seeking help to free her late husband's eight million dollars which are frozen—she offers to give you half if you send her your banking information—delete. Easy choice.

Other choices we make in life are more difficult. *Should I marry? Who will I marry? What career will I pursue? Should I have kids? Where will I live?*

But the most important choice anyone will ever make is the one Moses laid before the Israelites. It's not a multiple choice. There are only two choices. They may choose life, or they may choose death. Moses said,

> See, today I have set before you life and prosperity, death and adversity. For I am commanding you today to love the Lord your God, to walk in His ways, and to keep His commands, statutes, and ordinances, so that you may live and multiply, and the Lord your God may bless you in the land you are entering to possess (30:15-16).

We're familiar with the phrase, "Drawing a line in the sand." God had done this, but the line in the sand was actually a river—the Jordan. It separated the Israelites from life and death. If they chose death, they would remain in the wilderness and die. But if they chose life, they would cross over the Jordan where all of God's promises would be fulfilled. Moses gave them the challenge, and then he even provided them the correct choice.

We've arrived at the climax of Moses' series of proclamations. Beginning with the next chapter, he places the mantle of leadership upon Joshua. What a dramatic conclusion to Moses' message to the people. This chapter was written by Moses, and the remaining chapters are written about Moses.

Visualize this 120-year-old prophet standing there, as strong as a young man. His white hair and beard moving with the wind. With the fire of God in his eyes, he raises his hands and shouts:

> I call heaven and earth as witnesses against you today that I have set before you life and death, blessing and curse. Choose life so that you and your descendants may live, love the Lord your God, obey Him, and remain faithful to Him. For He is your life, and He will prolong your life in the land the Lord swore to give to your fathers Abraham, Isaac, and Jacob (30:19-20).

Why do you think some of the most important decisions in our lives require a step of faith?

» LEARNING ACTIVITY

TWO CHOICES

Moses presented two choices to the people. These are the same two choices presented to each of us. Which do you choose:

__I choose LIFE __I choose DEATH

A CLOSER LOOK

Jesus Is Our Life

We face the same life-or-death choice Moses gave the multitude. We can choose to accept God's offer of eternal life through Jesus. Or we can choose to reject His gracious offer. There are no other choices.

According to Ephesians 1, "He chose us in Him, before the foundation of the world, to be holy and blameless in His sight. In love He predestined us to be adopted through Jesus Christ for Himself, according to His favor and will" (Eph. 1:4-5). God chose us before we chose Him. In His perfect foreknowledge, He sees who will choose Him, and those are the elect.

The most important choice you'll ever make is how you respond to God's offer of salvation. Like Moses' offer, it is a choice of life or death. The Bible says, "The one who believes in the Son has eternal life, but the one who refuses to believe in the Son will not see life; instead, the wrath of God remains on him" (John 3:36).

1. Mark Twain, *Innocents Abroad* (London: Wordsworth Editions Limited, 2010), 313,360.

CHAPTER 8

GOD'S PEOPLE HAVE A SECURE FUTURE

DEUTERONOMY 31–34

There is something notable about last words. When famous people have approached death, their words have been recorded. John Sedgwick was a major general in the Union Army in the American Civil War. At the battle of Spotsylvania Court House in May 1864, Sedgwick was deploying his men to face the enemy. His troops were ducking down for cover from the occasional shots from Confederate snipers. General Sedgwick rallied his men and said, "They couldn't hit an elephant at this distance." Those were his last words because moments later, a sniper's bullet ended his life.

The Roman Emperor, Julian, was known as Julian the Apostate because he devoted his life attempting to reverse Constantine's endorsement of Christianity. Julian was wounded at the Battle of Samarra on June 26, A.D. 363. Three days later, a major hemorrhage occurred and the emperor died that night. Just before he died, his last words were, "You have won, Galilean."

In this final section of Deuteronomy, we find the last words of Moses. A great deal of the Bible to this point has been about Moses. He had been a key leader since the time the Israelites came out of the land of Egypt. He gave us a record of the 120 years of his life. As he prepared to die, he proclaimed both warnings and blessings to the generation poised to claim the promised land.

What were Jesus' recorded last words before He died? Before He ascended into heaven?

TIME FOR A NEW LEADER (DEUT. 31:1-23)

One thing that makes America a great nation is the orderly transfer of presidential power. During the election, the different candidates and parties are in attack mode. But when a new president is inaugurated, cooperation and courtesy are the orders of the day. This assures the population, and the world, that America is secure in its leadership. In the same way, Moses transferred leadership authority to Joshua.

It must have been a sad day when Moses announced to the Israelites that he would no longer be their leader. With great sadness, he informed them that he would not be accompanying them into Canaan. He was the only leader this generation had known. After their initial sorrow, their next emotion was probably fear. You can almost hear the whispered question that spread among the camp, "How will we ever make it without Moses?"

But Moses reassured the people by telling them that Yahweh was their true Leader, and He would never leave them. He said:

> The Lord your God is the One who will cross ahead of you. He will destroy these nations before you, and you will drive them out ... Be strong and courageous; don't be terrified or afraid of them. For it is the Lord your God who goes with you; He will not leave you or forsake you (31:3,6).

We sometimes face challenges that we fear are beyond our capabilities. It is in those times, that God reassures us His power and presence is available to sustain us. Human leaders come and go, but God has promised that He will never leave us. God says, "I will never leave you or forsake you. Therefore, we may boldly say: 'The Lord is my helper; I will not be afraid. What can man do to me?'" (Heb. 13:5-6).

We sometimes face challenges that we fear are beyond our capabilities.

In addition, Moses reassured the people by announcing that he was handing human leadership over to Joshua. "Moses then summoned Joshua and said to him in the sight of all Israel, 'Be strong and courageous, for you will go with this people into the land the Lord swore to give to their fathers. You will enable them to take possession of it'" (Deut. 31:7). God repeated this encouragement to be strong and courageous to Joshua as he assumed leadership (Josh. 1:6,9,18).

How well do you handle change?

How does it strengthen your faith to know that God will never forsake you?

» LEARNING ACTIVITY

GOD'S LEADER

MOSES	JOSHUA
Born in Egypt during slavery	Born in Egypt during slavery
Name means "drawn out of the water"	Name means "Yahweh delivered"
Family line of Levi	Family line of Ephraim
Raised in Pharaoh's house	Raised with the Israelite slaves
Called by God to lead the Israelites	Called by God to succeed Moses
Called by God at the burning bush	Called by God through Moses
God's instrument to confront Pharaoh	One of the twelve spies to the promise land
Believed God would provide the promised land	Believed God would provide the promised land
Servant of God	Servant/Assistant to Moses; Servant of God
Deliverer of God's Ten Commandments	General of Israelite forces
At his death, challenged the people to remain committed to God	At his death, challenged the people to remain committed to God

MOSES' FINAL WARNING (DEUT. 31:24–32:47)

The question is often raised about how much of the Pentateuch Moses actually wrote. Some liberal scholars suggest that Moses didn't write any of it. However, this passage makes it clear that Moses actually had a part of writing down the Law. We read:

> When Moses had finished writing down on a scroll every single word of this law, he commanded the Levites who carried the ark of the LORD's covenant, "Take this book of the law and place it beside the ark of the covenant of the LORD your God so that it may remain there as a witness against you" (31:24-26).

When you study the words of Jesus, you discover that He believed that Moses wrote at least a portion of the Law. On one occasion He was speaking to the Jewish leaders in Jerusalem. He said, "If you believed Moses, you would believe Me, because he wrote about Me. But if you don't believe his writings, how will you believe My words?" (John 5:46-47). On the first Easter afternoon, Jesus was walking with two disciples on the road to Emmaus. Luke records, "Beginning with Moses and all the Prophets, He interpreted for them the things concerning Himself in all the Scriptures" (Luke 24:27).

After Moses placed a copy of the written Law beside the ark of the covenant, he called for the leaders of the Israelites to gather before him to hear his final warning.

Deuteronomy 32 is often called the "Song of Moses." It should probably be identified as the "Sermon of Moses." And like many sermons, Moses had an introduction, three main points, a strong conclusion, and then he gave the invitation.

In the introduction (32:1-4), he began by exalting the greatness of God. That's a great way for every sermon to begin. He said, "For I will proclaim Yahweh's name. Declare the greatness of our God! The Rock—His work is perfect; all His ways are entirely just. A faithful God, without prejudice, He is righteous and true" (32:3-4).

In the first point of the message (32:5-14), Moses recounted how God had brought the Israelites from bondage into liberty. He employed the beautiful imagery of how God cares for the Israelites the way an eagle hovers over his young.

In the second main point of the sermon (32:15-18), Moses pointed out how Israel rejected God's gracious care. He called Israel "Jeshurun" which means "Upright one." He might have even been using the term sarcastically, because Israel had been anything but upright. He said, "Jeshurun became fat and rebelled ... He abandoned the God who made him and scorned the Rock of his salvation" (32:15).

In the third, and climatic point (32:19-42), it is no longer Moses speaking; instead God spoke through Moses. And what He said wasn't pleasant. God announced,

> They have provoked My jealousy with their so-called gods; they have enraged Me with their worthless idols. So I will provoke their jealousy with an inferior people; I will enrage them with a foolish nation (32:21).

In Romans 12:9, the apostle Paul challenged believers to refrain from taking vengeance. Then he quoted God's words spoken to the Israelites, "Vengeance belongs to Me; I will repay. In time their foot will slip, for their day of disaster is near, and their doom is coming quickly" (32:35).

In the conclusion of the sermon (32:43), Moses ended with a call for the nations to rejoice because God will purify His land and His people. After the sermon, Moses extended the invitation to the people. He said to them,

> Take to heart all these words I am giving as a warning to you today, so that you may command your children to carefully follow all the words of this law. For they are not meaningless words to you but they are your life, and by them you will live long in the land you are crossing the Jordan to possess (32:46-47).

Moses said that these words weren't just empty sayings. Instead they are words that will give them life. God's Word still gives us life. One of my favorite songs as a child said, "Sing them over again to me; Wonderful words of life; Let me more of their beauty see; Wonderful words of life. Words of life and beauty; Teach me faith and duty. Beautiful words, wonderful words, Wonderful words of life."[1]

Like the Israelites, how can you "take to heart" the truths in God's Word?

How does God's Word give us "life"?

MOSES' DEATH AND DISAPPOINTMENT (DEUT. 32:48-52)

Would you live your life any differently if you know for certain that you would die on a certain day? Other than a convicted killer on death row, none of us know exactly how or when we're going to die. But God favored Moses by telling him that he would soon die. God said:

> Go up Mount Nebo in the Abarim range in the land of Moab, across from Jericho, and view the land of Canaan I am giving

Left: Mount Nebo, rising 3,300 feet at the northeastern end of the Dead Sea. According to Scripture, Moses died on Nebo. At the crest you can see a modern sculpture commemorating Moses placing a brass serpent on a pole.

ILLUSTRATOR PHOTO/ BRENT BRUCE (60/8086)

> the Israelites as a possession. Then you will die on the mountain that you go up, and you will be gathered to your people (32:49-50).

Moses is a great example to us of how to deal with disappointment. His entire life's dream was to lead the Israelites into the promised land. But God told him that, like Aaron, he wouldn't be able to fulfill that dream. The reason? God said, "For both of you broke faith with Me among the Israelites at the waters of Meribath-kadesh in the Wilderness of Zin by failing to treat Me as holy in their presence" (32:51).

Moses is a great example to us of how to deal with disappointment.

Let's rewind to what happened that caused Moses to forfeit his dream of entering Canaan. As God led the Israelites through the wilderness, they were always in desperate need of water. In Exodus 17, God said to Moses, "Take the staff you struck the Nile with in your hand and go. I am going to stand there in front of you on the rock at Horeb; when you hit the rock, water will come out of it and the people will drink" (Ex. 17:5-6). Moses obeyed the Lord and water came from the rock.

However, years later when they were still in need of water, God gave Moses a different command. He said, "Take the staff and assemble the community. You and your brother Aaron are to speak to the rock while they watch, and it will yield its water" (Num. 20:8).

By this time, Moses was impatient and angry with the people because of their constant rebellion and complaining. He said, "Listen, you rebels! Must we bring water out of this rock for you?" Then Moses raised his hand and struck the rock twice with his staff, so that a great amount of water gushed out" (Num. 20:10-11).

The Lord gave them water, even though Moses disobeyed. But then God said, "Because you did not trust Me to show My holiness in the sight of the Israelites, you will not bring this assembly into the land I have given them" (Num. 20:12).

When we read those words, we're tempted to object and say, "What? Just for that one little act of disobedience? And yet all those rebellious people got to go in? That doesn't seem fair!"

There are several important lessons that can be learned from the rock incident. First, God places a higher standard upon His leaders. Moses had a special position as God's leader. The Bible says, "The Lord spoke with Moses face to face, just as a man speaks with his friend" (Ex. 33:11). Moses knew God more intimately than anyone else in the camp, so he was held to a higher level of accountability. Those of us who are leaders need to remember the warning of

James: "Not many should become teachers, my brothers, knowing that we will receive a stricter judgment" (Jas. 3:1).

A second lesson we learn is that God doesn't share His glory. Moses made it appear that he was the one who was causing the water to flow out of the rock. God rebuked Moses because he didn't reveal His holiness to the people. Instead, Moses was "hogging the limelight." God said through His prophet, Isaiah, "I am Yahweh, that is My name; I will not give My glory to another or My praise to idols" (Isa. 42:8).

Those of us who serve the Lord must be careful to give God all the glory and credit for anything good in our lives.

A final reason why Moses lost the chance of a lifetime is that God knew he didn't possess the right disposition to lead them into Israel. We have some indications that Moses had a problem with anger. He murdered an Egyptian earlier in his life—an act of angry violence. There in the desert he lost his temper again. He said, "You rebels!" But the Hebrew word is somewhat stronger—almost like he was calling them a dirty name. And he didn't just strike the rock once—he hit it twice. You can easily imagine him whacking the rock as his anger boiled over.

God needed a leader who would obey Him completely and not lose his cool. In a few weeks they would be attacking Jericho, the most heavily fortified city in the ancient world. God would direct Joshua to lead the people to walk around the city for seven days, and on the seventh day to walk around it seven times. If hot-tempered, impulsive Moses couldn't follow God's directions to speak to a rock, he might not have been able to carry out that plan of walking around the city. Who knows? He might have dashed up to the main gate of Jericho and started whacking away with his stick!

When was a time you were confused about something God did not allow you to have or experience?

What can you do to affirm your faith in God's Word even when you don't understand His ways? Explain.

» LEARNING ACTIVITY

YOU DID NOT TREAT ME AS HOLY

The verdict rendered to Moses was that Moses did not treat God "as holy in their presence" (Deut. 32:51). What are some ways that believers today fail to treat or represent God as holy in the presence of others?

BLESSINGS FOR GOD'S PEOPLE (DEUT. 33:1-29)

Deuteronomy 33 is a wonderful example of Hebrew poetry in which Moses addressed each one of the twelve tribes of Israel. He gave each one a particular blessing to sustain them as they entered the Promised Land. You can think of this as Moses' last will and testament.

One of the interesting promises was given to Asher, which is the land that borders the Mediterranean Sea around current day Haifa.

Moses predicted, "Most blessed of sons is Asher; let him be favored by his brothers, and let him bathe his feet in oil" (33:24, NIV). In my many trips to Israel, my Israeli friends have expressed, with a wry sense of irony, that God blessed the surrounding Arab nations with rich oil reserves and only gave rocks to Israel. However, according to the *Bloomberg* report (July 18, 2013), a huge crude oil reserve exists off the coast of Haifa. The deepest oil drilled in the Mediterranean sea is called the Leviathan well, which will drill 6,500 meters below the seabed. The strata may have as much as 1.5 billion barrels of crude oil. The oil-bearing strata are believed to be beneath the gas-bearing strata. Perhaps, finally, the descendants of Asher will bathe their feet in oil!

After Moses devotes a separate stanza to each tribe, he concludes with a summary of the entire faith and hope of Israel, concentrated in a few powerful words. They are also some of the most beautiful words ever attributed to him.

Elisabeth Elliot was the widow of Jim Elliot who was killed by the Auca Indians in 1956. She returned to Ecuador to minister to the same tribe that had made her a widow. She later returned to the U.S. and had an active speaking and writing ministry. For 13 years she had a radio program called "Gateway to Joy." She opened every broadcast with the same words. She said, "You are loved with an everlasting love. And underneath are the everlasting arms."

Most of us are familiar with the wonderful hymn that says, "Leaning on the everlasting arms." Did you know that great promise is found in Deuteronomy 33?

Moses' last words were, "There is none like the God of , who rides the heavens to your aid, the clouds in His majesty. The God of old is your dwelling place, and underneath are the everlasting arms" (33:26-27).

A naturalist was doing a study of the parenting skills of eagles. He wrote about observing that a mother eagle had built her nest on a ledge of rock, a rock that jutted out over the steep and dangerous precipice. One day she laid four eggs, and she and her mate sat on them until they hatched. Then began the task of feeding. Both parents were involved in the endless search for field-mice and the like to fill four beaks which never seemed satisfied.

Some days later, returning to her nest, the mother only saw three eaglets. Clinging to the edge of the rock with all its might was one of her babies—below it a fall of more than 1,000 feet. It could not fly yet, and if it fell, it would probably die.

Screeching, the mother flew toward her off spring, but as she flew, the baby's strength ran out, and it fell from the ledge. As it fell the mother swooped low beneath the jutting rock, her strong wings spread wide to break the baby's fall, and then she caught it in her talons and glided with her little one, safely back to its nest.

Perhaps that's the picture Moses had in mind when he told the Israelites that "underneath are the everlasting arms." That's also a truth that each of us can claim. We may be experiencing weakness, faintness, pain, or sorrow—but we can never sink below His everlasting arms.

We can never sink below His everlasting arms.

When was a time you felt God upholding you with His everlasting arms?

What do you learn about yourself and about God when you trust Him completely in difficult circumstances?

GOD'S LEADER GOES HOME (DEUT. 34:1-9)

The original scrolls of the Bible didn't have all the divisions that we have for chapters, verses, and even books. Some scholars have noted that this final chapter of Deuteronomy was penned by Joshua, and should actually be the first chapter of Joshua. Where the narrative belongs is not as important as what we learn.

Moses climbed to the top of Mount Pisgah and the Lord showed him the entire land of Canaan—from Gilead in the south to Dan in the north. This was a supernatural panorama that God offered Moses, because it is physically impossible to stand on the mountains of Nebo and see the entire length of the promised land. Then God called Moses home. The Bible says:

> So Moses the servant of the LORD died there in the land of Moab, as the LORD had said. He buried him in the valley in the land of Moab facing Beth-peor, and no one to this day knows where his grave is. Moses was 120 years old when he died; his eyes were not weak, and his vitality had not left him (34:5-7).

It appears that Moses died alone. The text indicates that God buried Moses. One translation says, "He died by the kiss of God." Perhaps God just kissed His friend and put him to sleep. Why was his grave unknown? Maybe because God knew that the Israelites might set up a shrine and worship their deceased leader.

In the New Testament Book of Jude, we are told a strange detail about Moses' corpse. Jude was writing about how false prophets reject spiritual authority. As a contrast to this attitude, he wrote, "Yet Michael the archangel, when he was disputing with the Devil in a debate about Moses' body, did not dare bring an abusive condemnation against him but said, 'The Lord rebuke you!'" (Jude 1:9).

Left: A Byzantine basilica was discovered in the 1930s atop Mount Nebo. Seen is a modern church that has been incorporated with the basilica remains and is known as the Memorial Church of Moses.

ILLUSTRATOR PHOTO/ BRENT BRUCE (60/8088)

Obeying rules will never bring us into the life of victory and blessing. Only Jesus can!

Many believe Satan tried to steal the body of Moses because he knew that God had better plans for Moses. Moses never set foot in the promised land during his 120 years of life. Yet, when we open our New Testament, we discover that when Jesus was transfigured before Peter, James, and John, Moses and Elijah appeared with Jesus. So, you see, Moses did finally get to the promised land. The Law could never bring Moses into the land of promise, but the Lord Jesus Christ could! The same is true for us. Obeying rules will never bring us into the life of victory and blessing. Only Jesus can!

How do you know for certain that "this life" is not all there is?

How does knowing you will one day inherit eternal life affect your daily life?

1. Words by Phillip Bliss, "Wonderful Words of Life," 1847, Public domain.

Two Ways to Earn Credit
for Studying LifeWay Christian Resources Material

Christian Growth Study Plan resources are available for course credit for personal growth and church leadership training.

Courses are designed as plans for personal spiritual growth and for training current and future church leaders. To receive credit, complete the book, material, or activity. Respond to the learning activities or attend group sessions, when applicable, and show your work to your pastor, staff member, or church leader. Then go to *www.lifeway.com/CGSP*, or call the toll-free number for instructions for receiving credit and your certificate of completion.

For information about studies in the Christian Growth Study Plan, refer to the current catalog online at the CGSP Web address. This program and certificate are free LifeWay services to you.

CONTACT INFORMATION:
Christian Growth Study Plan
One LifeWay Plaza, MSN 117
Nashville, TN 37234
CGSP info line 1-800-968-5519
www.lifeway.com/CGSP
To order resources 1-800-485-2772

Need a CEU?

Receive Continuing Education Units (CEUs) when you complete group Bible studies by your favorite LifeWay authors.

Some studies are approved by the Association of Christian Schools International (ACSI) for CEU credits. Do you need to renew your Christian school teaching certificate? Gather a group of teachers or neighbors and complete one of the approved studies. Then go to *www.lifeway.com/CEU* to submit a request form or to find a list of ACSI-approved LifeWay studies and conferences. Book studies must be completed in a group setting. Online courses approved for ACSI credit are also noted on the course list. The administrative cost of each CEU certificate is only $10 per course.

CONTACT INFORMATION:
CEU Coordinator
One LifeWay Plaza, MSN 150
Nashville, TN 37234
Info line 1-800-968-5519
www.lifeway.com/CEU